JURISFICTIONS

JURISFICTIONS

Little Fantasies Raising Deeper Questions
about the Nature of Law

J. STANLEY MCQUADE
ART PATTY LUDWIG JUNG

 ARCHWAY
PUBLISHING

Archway Publishing books may be ordered through booksellers or by contacting:

Archway Publishing
1663 Liberty Drive
Bloomington, IN 47403
www.archwaypublishing.com
1 (888) 242-5904

ISBN: 978-1-4808-3435-4 (sc)
ISBN: 978-1-4808-3436-1 (e)

Library of Congress Control Number: 2016947847

Print information available on the last page.

Archway Publishing rev. date: 08/30/2016

CONTENTS

DEDICATION

To Founding Dean F. Leary Davis, a friend and adviser
over many years, who not only tolerated my Irish madnesses
but actively encouraged them. Otherwise this book would
probably never have been written much less published

PREFACE TO JURISFICTIONS

Plato one of the greatest, if not the greatest teacher of Philosophy, said that learning should be fun, and he was also partial to myths and little stories to get over some serious truths. My first idea in creating the fictions was to have a little fun with my students, and it was fun writing these little fantasies. But a deeper purpose soon became apparent, namely to sneak into their minds some deeper questions about important founding principles of the law.

All the characters, save one, are entirely fictitious and bear no resemblance to anyone living or dead.

The exception is Rev. Samuel McWaddy who is myself: my name was so pronounced by a baggage handler in a European hotel. I am an orthodox and enthusiastic disciple of the great John Wesley, but with a little wicked sense of humor that gets out of hand occasionally.

There was no prototype whatsoever for Count Nicholai Dimski, I never moved in such exalted circles, but we have all met bright people with strange ideas, and the link of science and mathematics with the law is a strong one. It began with Plato, continued throughout the middle ages, declined somewhat with Austin's descriptive jurisprudence, revived with the Legal Realist's fascination with statistics; and I think it is high time that it came full circle (no pun intended) with Frege's game theory of mathematics.

The interpretative notes represent the considerable maturing of my opinions from those featured in the original publication of Jurisfictions some thirty or so years ago. The fictions are closely linked with the more serious notes which follow. The notes are intended to correct and supplement the ubiquitous distortions of the fictions. But the fictions play an important role, for error and misunderstanding are excellent tools for accurately communicating the truth.

PART ONE

HOW LAW SHOULD
BE ORGANIZED

Codes v. Common Law

OUR AUTHOR

John Ignatius O'Flynn hard at work

Well-known "character" about town, O'Flynn "studied" law for one year but apparently was more active in the literary and debating society and the drama circle than in his studies. He was thrown out of law school after failing his first year exams for the third time on the grounds that, like necessity, he knew no law. O'Flynn did not agree and seeking for some better way to communicate his valuable insights on law, he took to the drama and produced a series of plays, all on legal themes - "Oedipus Lex", "Law and Peace", "MacDeath", etc. These works are rather long and filled with inaccuracies. "Napoleon's Farewell To Berlin", one of the earliest of these plays, has the additional disadvantage that the author felt obliged to render the dialogue in the vernacular of the back streets of Dublin (his "begob" and "begorrah" period). This may be a little puzzling to American or English readers and his fellow Dubliners are not exactly crazy about it either.

The justification for including some extracts from his writings here is the belief that distortion and error, if gross enough, can be a wonderful stimulus to thinking and a useful starting point for enquiry.

O'Flynn supported himself during his dramatic days by tending bar at McGlade's tavern but eventually became a lawyer by one of the circuitous routes which were then available in England and Ireland. My understanding is that he is quite a capable lawyer though a scintilla of the old gleam still remains in his eye

NAPOLEON'S FAREWELL TO BERLIN

Napoleon saying good bye to Berlin

Napoleon's Farewell to Berlin

A Historical Tragedy
By
John Ignatius O'Flynn, L.

Dramats Personae

Napoleon
Professor Thibaut
Elector of Schlieswig-Holstein
Professor Savigny
Elector of Holswig-Schliestein
Elector of Saxe-Coburg
King of Prussia
Elector of Cobe-Saxeburg
Emperor of Austria
Little man (Jacob Hoffa)

ACT I

SCENE. - *The Steps of the Ratkeller (Town hall) in Berlin*

Napoleon has just lost a battle and is about to be retired to Elba or St. Helena or somewhere[1] He is saying farewell to a bunch of assembled dignitaries and bigwigs from various petty German states.

Napoleon: I have, as the introduction remarks, just lost a battle. If some of me marshals had been a bit quicker and the Prooshians a bit slower, it might have been a different story, but that's all water under the bridge. Now I've got to hand in the key of me desk and retire. So I bid youse farewell, but before I go there's one little matter weighin' on me mind that I'd like ye to help me on. Yez'll remember I'm sure the code of law I've been imposin' on yez all for the last ten years or so. It's got me own name on it though I did get a little help from oul' doctor Potter.[2] Well, it's the only book I ever wrote and I would like to be remembered by it, so I am hopin' that when I'm chewin' me nails out in St. Helena or wherever, that you'll keep it goin' in the courts and law schools because I'm sure I'll need the royalties.

Elector of Schlieswig-Holstein: Three cheers for Napoleon, Hip Hip . . .

[*No response at first, but Napoleon eyes them all very hard and as he hasn't quite retired yet, they give him a standing ovulation*]

Napoleon: Thank yez all and good luck; don't forget me book.

[*Retires with Marshals and aides and what-not*]

Elector of Holswig-Schliestein: [*Shaking his fist*] Three cheers indeed! Good riddance I say, and I'll tell yez right now we're not usin' his book in my bailiwick. Maybe I'll write me own.

---

[1] O'Flynn, like most Irishmen, had no head for dates, or, for that matter, for facts.

[2] Presumably Joseph Pothier, the distinguished French jurist. The truth is the other way round. Pothier wrote most of the code. Napoleon's help was entirely administrative and financial

[*Laughter*]

King of Prussia: Well, as ye may be aware, we have had our own Prussian code ready for some time, and yez can be sure it's goin' intil effect this minute.

Emperor of Austria: Same here.

[*Pandemonium*]

Elector of Schlieswig-Holstein: Order! Order! Gintlemen, kindly remember that yez are rulers and potentates and what-not and supposed till set an example.

[*They simmer down*]

Thank ye kindly. Now that his nibs is gone we have to decide what to do. Let's have a show of hands. All in favor of keeping Napoleon's Code . . .

[*No hands*]

I thought not - any other ideas?

Emperor of Austria: Why not use my code?

King of Prussia: Why not use mine? It's not too big, and it has a nice title - I call it the *Landrecht*.

Elector of Holswig-Schliestein: *(Noted as a heavy wit)* Schiffrecht[3] might be closer to the mark.

[*Blows and coarse insults all around*]

Elector of Schlieswig-Holstein: Order! Order! Let's hear what Professor Thibaut has to say. I understand he is a fellow of the Berlin Academy.

---

[3] O'Flynn described this as a Deutchespun

All: *(Sing.)* And he's a jolly good fellow, *etc.*

*[**Laughter and cries of "order". They eventually settle down**]*

Professor Thibaut of Berlin: Yer worships, I want to start by congratulatin' yez all on rejectin' Napoleon's Code, because it's French and we're Germans. I need hardly remind you of the difference. We eat sauerkraut and wiener-schnitzel like civilized human bein's; we don't eat frogs. So it's obvious that we need a different law. Now we Germans should have one single law because it's very awkward to go from one state to another and have to learn a new set of laws everywhere ye go. And it's the divil' to teach them all in law school, I promise you. There should be only one law then: but which law? I have a suggestion to make. I have looked at the Prussian and Austrian Codes, and they are very nice indeed, but what we really need is a new German code made for us all. And we could have one in no time. Professor Pothier made one for Napoleon, and I'm sure (Ahem!) that I could find somebody to make you one right here in Berlin.

Elector of Schlieswig-Holstein: Very good idea, but I see Professor Savigny here, and I wonder if our distinguished professor of Roman Law would care to say a few words?

Savigny: I certainly would. I teetotally disagree with Thibaut. We've just managed to get rid of one code, yet here we are tryin' to saddle ourselves with another one. There never was a good code yet, and there never will be. Even if Thibaut was as smart as he thinks he is, it would take a hundred of him to make the code. It would be years out of date before it reached the printers and it wouldn't fit all the cases that would come up. To the hinges[4] with codes, I say, let the judges make the law up as they go along.

Professor Thibaut: The judges you say! Do you think they're smarter than us professors?

---

[4]   Abbreviation for the hinges of Hades, i.e. the perpetual pit.

Savigny: No, av coorse not, but they don't have to be. They only have to decide one case at a time. That way the law can grow slowly to fit the feelins' of the people,[5] like the skin on a potato.

Professor Thibaut: Aber Herr Hauptman wass willen sie auf der begriffungenspunct and viel zu viel flexibilitischung fur unser sicher gut.[6]

Savigny: Natürlich.

Elector of Saxe-Coburg: Gintlemen, this has been a very interesting discussion so far as I could follow it, but some of us have a few questions to ask of a practical nature. And my first question is to Professor Thibaut. Could you tell me sor, if we were to use your code, who gets the royalties?

Professor Thibaut: I'll just look and see **[he consults his code]** Meself.

Elector of Saxe-Coburg: [*Thoughtfully*] Hm!

Elector of Cobe-Saxeburg: Professor Savigny, if we left the law makin' to the judges, who would appoint the judges?

Savigny: Why, the electors and princes, av coorse.

Elector of Cobe-Saxeburg: And we could collect the court costs?

Savigny: Natürlich.

Elector of Cobe-Saxeburg: *(Equally thoughtfully)* **Hmm.**

Professor Thibaut: I have a question or two for my colleague also. savvykinder,[7] would we get to teach the judges?

---

[5] O'Flynn's version of Savigny's famous *volksgeist*

[6] I gather that this is intended to represent a highly technical, and therefore untranslatable discussion in German about the respective merits of judge-made law and codes. All the well worn points about the alleged flexibility of the one and the certainty of the other are present in the text, expressly or by implication.

[7] I gather that this is intended to be the German equivalent of "Savigny-baby"

Savigny: Jawohl.

Professor Thibaut: And do you suppose that if they had a particularly tough case, they would call us in to consult, for a fee, av coorse?

Savigny: Probablische.

Professor Thibaut: [*Extremely thoughtfully*] Hmmmmm.

[*Enter nasty little man with a straggly beard and little affinity for soap and water.*]

Little man: Ich bin der secretary von der transportishe and generalischewerkersunion. Mein namen ist Jacob Hoffa.[8]

Savigny: Who?

Elector of Saxe-Coburg: He is a peasant leader, Professor. They are revolting.

Savigny: Quite.

Hoffa: Did I understand you to say that the judges would make the law to suit the spirit of the people?

Savigny: Correctishe.

Hoffa: Would the people be mostly us peasants

Savigny: Natürlich., there are rather a lot of you.

Hoffa: [*Very thoughtfully*] Hmmm

Elector of Schlieswig-Holstein: If I have been following this discussion correctische, the consensus of the meeting is in favor of Professor

---

[8] O'Flunn's pigeon German again, but very easily translated.

Savigny's proposal by four "Hmmms" to nothing. Why don't we make it unanimous?

All: [in four part harmony]

Hmmmmmmmmmmmmmmmmmmmmmmmmmmmminmnimmmmmmmm!

THE END

COMMENT

1. This fiction is ostensibly about Napoleon and his code: but in the background is the mathematician and philosopher, Rene Descartes. Descartes threw away his law books in disgust and proposed that a simple code could be created, out of the air as it were, consisting of sensible and clear rules that could be used to avoid and resolve disputes without any need for lawyers. This proposal was popular with the revolutionaries of France in the late eighteenth century. They had suffered much from lawyers, who largely functioned as supporters of the oppressive aristocrats. To Napoleon, supporting (as he thought) this idea, was one of his major claims to be a liberator of the common people.[9]

2. This notion spread like wildfire as a leading principle in a new order of things and continued to be influential after the defeat and departure of Napoleon. European countries until Napoleon had been divided up into minor princedoms each with their own monarchs and laws. Following Napoleon, there was a great surge of nationalism in Germany Italy and Spain with the idea that there should be one people, one government, one language and one law. But the question was "which law"? A return to the modern Roman law was one suggestion, some even suggested going back to the old

---

[9] The other was the notion of meritocracy, that promotion and advancement should be based on merit not family connection. He boasted that every soldier in his army carried a field marshal's baton in his haversack. This was political dynamite at the time, so that all the surrounding nations combined in an attempt to snuff it out.

customary legal system (totally obsolete). But frequently this new law, was envisaged as a code in the manner of Descartes, a clear and understandable collection of laws which anyone could read and understand and which would not require lawyers to interpret and apply it. This proposal has been followed more or less in about half the legal jurisdictions in the world.[10]

3. Professor Thibaut, a colleague of Savigny in Berlin, offered to produce such a code and it was his proposal that led Savigny to write his famous monograph on our capacity for jurisprudence and legislation, which delayed the production of the German code for some eighty years.

4. Savigny's objections to the codification proposal are well known: its promises of clarity and ease of administration were specious and the notion that it would not need lawyers to manage it was clearly wrong. However, often overlooked, are his own proposals for the reform of the law; and these are worth considering.

5. Savigny was by no means a legal conservative. He was well aware of the need to continually modernize and otherwise improve the existing law. But his method has not received the attention it deserves. His school of thought is generally known as historical jurisprudence[11] and his work stimulated a great surge of interest in the history of the law, notably in Cambridge, where great scholars, for example Sir William Maitland and Sir Frederick Pollock, were attracted to the historical investigation of law. But Savigny's concern was not just with understanding the law but going further to use historical investigation as a procedure to update it and improve it. His recipe was to take a rule of law and trace it back to its origins and see if and how it fitted into the culture of that time; and then move forward and see how things may have changed and whether the rule might still function well in current society or at least be modified to do so[12]. This might seem a cumbersome way to go about law reform

---

[10] They cheat of course. There is always a trained lawyer at the lay judge's elbow to keep the court on track.

[11] He encouraged hiss research assistants, he Brothers Grimm, to study German folk lore as a way of gaining insight into German culture (the volksgeist).

[12] Savigny's approach to law should more properly be called Sociological Jurisprudence.

but the basic idea is simple: presumably when the law was created it filled some purpose in society: so we must go on to ask whether that purpose still exists and whether the law needs to be tweaked some in order to serve current needs and objectives

6. Savigny's idea of legal science is also worth considering. His models in this regard were the jurisconsults of ancient Rome. They did not bother themselves much with precisely defining legal terms but rather tried to identify the major principles and policies that created and supported the law. The expert jurist, according to Savigny, would know how to see these principles in the particular cases and, conversely, know how to apply the principles to resolve current cases.

7. His ideas here seem to have imprinted themselves in European legal thought, probably due to the massive labors of Savigny and his associates to modernize Roman law by his historical method so that it could be used in formulating the later German code.

8. These ideas can be seen in practice by contrasting the directives of the European Union with the Restatements and Model Uniform Statutes produced in America. Anglo-American legal productions are summaries of the existing law. They are very lengthy and detailed and filled out with references to authoritative cases. The European model on the other hand is considerably shorter. The Products Liability directive is only a few pages long and does not include references to case law. Case law interpreting the code can be and is extensive and lawyers have to pay attention to it, but it is persuasive only rather than binding. I see great merit in this approach, not least because it focuses attention on the purposes and values which should direct the interpretation of laws[13].

9. Savigny's pamphlet contains a number of other notions which are of merit. One of these is his idea of the organization of the legal profession into a collegium, like the legal fraternities of ancient Rome, where the members of a profession join together to promote a scientific approach to their work, which is best done by their working together. Savigny is most insistent that the great giants

---

[13] This approach accords well with the basic principle of Wittgenstein's later understanding of how purpose controls the application of word games. We must understand a joke differently from a command or a factual statement.

of science do not appear out of the air, but are the product of a communal undertaking. The apples are the product of the tree and of its branches, they do not fall from heaven in completed form.

10. Another useful set of notions found in his pamphlet is his statement of the preconditions required for a set of laws, whether code or otherwise, to come into being and to function. These conditions are:

(i)   A stable society for in social chaos there can be no law:

(ii)   There must be a considerable body of law already in place, for one cannot readily start from nothing:

(iii) There must be a trained legal profession, for Savigny insists, and it seems sensible, that the major role in formulating or amending laws involves the legal profession. This must be so since new laws must be fitted into the law already in place; and the lawyers are the most obvious people to do this. They will also be needed to interpret and apply it.

(iv)   His final prerequisite for legal science is an adequate technical language, which again fits in well with modern linguistic logic ideas (See later Fictions *Underside* and *The Ballet of the Books*).

11. The importance of Savigny, so evident in the nineteenth century, has faded away almost to nothing. He has indeed been called the forgotten man. This may be due to the fact that his proposals are so eminently sensible that they no longer attract attention. He might, it has been suggested, have fared better if he had danced up and down, foamed at the mouth and said a few more controversial things. But be that as it may, many of the things that he said are currently of interest and have considerable promise for contemporary law.. His work might indeed be overdue for a rerun in the present legal scene, especially since globalization of the law is bringing the common law increasingly into contact with the Civil law in Europe and most other parts of the world.

PART TWO

THE BUSINESS OF THE LAWYER - DESCRIPTIVE JURISPRUDENCE.

John Austin and the descriptive science of law

OUR AUTHOR

Michael Joseph O'Houlihan, LL.D.

Professor of Law at the old University of Ireland in the days of few students and even fewer professors. "Mad Mike," as he was affectionately called, taught Jurisprudence, Torts, Contracts, Property, Equity, Evidence, Pleading and Practice, Commercial Law, International Law (both public and private) and Bills of Exchange. The Reader[14], the Dean, and a few adjunct professors taught the remainder. He bitterly resented being retired at the statutory age and delighted in remarking that they had to hire three men to do his work. He remained in the environs of the university and supported himself by giving "grinds" (tutoring) to law students who were not doing very well. He enjoyed the company of his students and was wont to go forth with them on Friday nights when they generally ended up in McGlade's tavern where he would often deliver what we might call public lectures at least in the sense that they were given in a public house. Mrs. O'Houlihan was invariably present whenever the Professor was holding forth (to keep an eye on him and also to act as his private secretary). She sat silent in the front row, like Madame Defarge at the tumbrils, reducing her husband's meandering remarks to sequential sentences as best she could. A few of these manuscripts have survived to bear testimony to the learning, critical acumen and erratic genius of the great O'Houlihan. Typical examples are, "Amputation of the foot - a return to stare descissis?" - and "Back to the rack - a modification of Miranda." The lecture included here, "The Law v. John Austin," was more or less an annual event given on the anniversary of the death of that great man. There were several versions of it, all uncomplimentary and unfavorable in the extreme. O'Houlihan's dislike of Austin was partly doctrinal and partly personal. His chagrin at his own modest fortunes was heightened by the thought of Austin's success, which O'Houlihan regarded as largely due to luck, in short to the fact that Austin happened to say his piece to the right

---

[14] Roughly equivalent to "associate professor" in the U.S..

people at the right time and place. O'Houlihan was never in doubt that he was saying the right thing. Since however, since he could not get it to the right people at the right time, he had to content himself with being at the right place, the "snug" at McGlade's *tavern*.

[*Cheers*]

The great O;Houlihan (with book and glass) in full flow

THE LAW V. JOHN AUSTIN

An Undecided Paternity Suit
By
Michael J. O'Houlihan, LL.D.,D.Litt.

The following manuscript was discovered among the papers of the late Professor Michael J. O'Houlihan of the Old University of Ireland. Like John Austin's work it appears to have been compiled posthumously by his wife who was a vigorous editor, especially remarkable in her dedication to proper English and her aversion to strong drink and bad language[15]. Her professor husband's approach to learned writing was singular, not to say peculiar. For instance, he did not believe in footnotes, which he referred to as "padding" and considered more or less a literary device to give the appearance of learning to what might otherwise be regarded as

---

[15] She insisted for example on substituting "-ing" for the normal "-in". No Irishman will say "doing" or 'going', certainly not in a public house.

trash. He was particularly averse to citing secondary authorities feeling no obligation, he said, to peddle the opinions of other people when he had plenty of his own. Such quotations and citations as he gives are systematically vague, and he generally located them by remarking that he had read them "somewhere or other." Indeed it is difficult to tell whether he really had read them anywhere or just made them up "out of his own head." But his arguments can usually stand on their own without them, and even if nobody ever said them, somebody should have and maybe somebody did!

Some of the peculiarities of this manuscript are explained by the fact that the professor spoke extemporaneously and that his wife and amanuensis, though an astute and well read lady, was not always familiar with the topic under discussion; also the Professor's speech was sometimes slurred as the evening progressed. I have tried to restore the original text as best I can; but since my hearing was also slurred at times, I am not sure myself in spots. But we can be certain that if he didn't say these things then he probably said something else.

O'Flynn [rising] Ladies and Gentlemen, tonight we are going to try a paternity suit. You will be the jury and I will be the judge summarizing the evidence and putting the issues to you.

Most paternity cases, including the present one, reach the court because somebody doesn't want to own up to fathering the child. This one is no exception. The child is the law as presently studied and practiced.

[points to a cradle containing a lot of law books]

John Austin has been accused of being its father. If he were here and had any sense he would deny the charge, so we will assume he pleads "not guilty" and present the evidence.

In modern paternity suits there are all sorts of blood tests to prove whether anybody was or was not the villain of the piece. These are not available in the present case so we will just have to do it in the old way, asking whether the party in question was around and available at the right time and whether the child looks as if it might be his.

First, let us look at the putative father. Who was he?

John Austin has been called "The Father of English Jurisprudence."[16] Mrs. Austin was presumably "The Mother of English Jurisprudence," but we will ignore that nasty allegation for present purposes. John Austin came from a good family and had a lot of friends, in short he had all the influence and pull that a fellow could wish for to make a go of it. It must be admitted that he had some talent too, in fact he was generally thought to have been a very smart fellow[17] indeed (though Mrs. Austin may well have been smarter)[18]. He was a very learned chap too, he had read a lot of philosophy books and knew something of classical Latin and Greek, history, and social sciences. Anything he didn't know himself he could always pick up in conversation at the dinner table with his omniscient friends, Bentham and the Mills. He started out in the army, where he learned about commands, no doubt.[19] He then switched to the law and became an equity draftsman.[20] He wrote a very nice hand and had the gift of the gab, so everybody assumed, with a lawyer brother who could no doubt give him lots of business, that he would be a big success. But he wasn't (he was a bit slow). So his friends got him a job as the first Law Professor in the new University they had started in London. However, he didn't do well there either.

He started with twenty six students and ended up with six, and since his salary was paid out of their fees he was obliged to quit; He got a job for a while drawing up a new constitution for Gibraltar[21] (no doubt a hard task).

[dutiful laughter]

But he quit there too and thereafter for the most part he just traveled around and did this and that. He was in Germany for a couple of years and met the great German jurist, Savigny. I have no idea how he supported

---

[16] By somebody or other

[17] The original was certainly "fella".

[18] Undoubtedly an insertion by Mrs O'Houlihan

[19] Austin's work has been described by critics as the jurisprudence of the drill sergeant.

[20] Dealing mostly with deeds and contracts and trusts.

[21] It was Malta but so what?

himself.[22] He was said to be in poor health, and maybe he was because eventually he died. He left heaps and heaps of papers, none of them anywhere near ready to be published. If it hadn't been for Mrs. Austin and John Stuart Mill (who sat through his classes to the bitter end) he would never have been heard of. But these two got together and put his lectures into a book called SIX LECTURES IN JURISPRUDENCE (they kept changing the title to make it sell). It was this book that made his reputation and changed the course of the law both in England and America. It was indeed the *fons et origo*[23] of all the disasters that have overtaken the law since. I would even characterize it as a veritable sperm bank for every abortive idea that has come into being in the profession from that day to this.

**[*Pandemonium. The Professor, choked with emotion, takes a stiff snort*].
[Someone refills his glass]**

Thank you. My humble apologies to the ladies present for that last and totally uncalled-for remark. You may think all this is a bit far fetched. Are you trying to tell me, you may say, that a sorry failure like this could do any harm with a book? Ah, but that's where you make your big mistake. Most of us do a little harm once in while, though mostly to ourselves.[24] A few people get up to general mayhem and carnage. But if you want to see real ruination, don't look at the people who go round thieving and burning and generally getting up to their knees in blood. The world suffers from such for a while, but it gets over them and they are soon forgotten. The ones that do the real harm are seemingly innocent and harmless people, like Austin, that write books telling other people how to do things. The power of poor advice is awesome to contemplate. I myself would surely this day be rich and famous and possibly even sober[25] had it not been for poor advice. Many of you have

---

[22] Mrs Austin contributed a great deal as she was a gifted translator of foreign books and much in demand.

[23] Fountain and source: very apt since Adam was described as the *fons et origo* of the human race.

[24] Reliable sources report that the Professor sighed deeply and wiped a tear from the corner of his eye

[25] The original was "single". Mrs. O'Houlihan's substitution is understandable

been the victims of bad advice, though you should have had more sense than to listen to your fellow students instead of me.[26]

And you may have noticed that the poorest students are the most eager to tell you how to do it. *Timeo Danaos et dona ferentes.*[27]So I warn you – never mind the warriors, fear the scholars. They write their little books and slip their little ideas into your innocent little heads, and there they germinate and take root and grow and before you know it you're up to your whatnot in weeds.

[more emotion. Another refill of the glass]

But I'm getting ahead of myself. Before I finally charge Austin with responsibility for the weeds, I had better hold out the seeds for your inspection. So let me present you with Austin's ideas - ladies and gentlemen of the jury I give you Exhibit A

[produces a copy of Austin's "The Province of Jurisprudence Determined" and waves it dramatically over his head before laying it on the table]

What did he say that was so terrible? Very simply this, that the study of the law should be **[dramatic pause]** scientific! That's not so awful, you say, we're all scientists now. True, but Austin changed the meaning of the word science - just like he changed the meaning of a whole lot of words. The big name in science then was Sir Isaac Newton and Sir Isaac knew exactly what he meant by science. Science, said he, is looking deeply and carefully into the mysteries of the creation. Note the "deeply". Sir Isaac also said [28]on another occasion that with all his knowledge he was just like a little boy wandering on the seashore picking up and admiring a shell here and there; but all the while the sea stretched over the horizon, and below the surface were fathomless depths. Note the "depths". All very humble and mysterious. And what does Mr. Austin have to say

---

[26] The professor's students were not the brightest in the class and were therefore very susceptible to influence from their more talented colleagues.

[27] "I fear the Greeks when they come bearing gifts". Priest Laocoon's warning the Trojans about the wooden horse.

[28] Somewhere or other

about that? Well, he had been doing a little reading in the philosopher Thomas Hobbes who didn't hold with all this deep mystery stuff. It smacked of the clergy, and old Tom wasn't over fond of the clergy. You can just see Tom taking Newton by the arm and sez he:[29]

"Isaac, you've got to forget all this 'over the horizon and down in the depths' stuff. 'Over the horizon' is for sailors and 'down in the depths' is for fish. All you'll get is either lost or drownded. Concentrate on the job in hand. Put those shells that you've got in your hand in order, and forget about the places you can't go and things you can't see."

"What do you mean, Tom?" sez Isaac.

"It's very simple," sez Tom, "in nature, one event follows another in an orderly way; day follows night, summer follows winter, B follows A, and I hope you follow me."

"Av coorse!" sez Newton.[30]

"So the business of a scientist is to look at the things takin' place around him and figure out which ones regularly follow one another - which is a B and which an A so to speak. Now there's no great mystery about that, is there?"

"No," sez Isaac, "it would seem not."

"Even your experiments," sez Tom, "work the same way."[31]

"How's that" sez Isaac

"Well, consider this pin to be an A and when I stick it into you, your guldher[32] will be a B."

---

[29] This kind of imaginary dialogue is a standard device among Irish orators.

[30] Good Elizabethan English. Shakespeare pronounced and spelt 'door' as 'dure', and so he should.

[31] Sir Isaac Newton did not generally do experiments but worked things out in his head.

[32] Irish for a loud yell.

[He jabs the pin into Isaac where it will do most good]

"Oww!" sez Isaac.

"You see," sez Tom, "A is followed by B."

"And your bloody nose will be C," sez Isaac, and rightly so.

So this was to be the new science. Surface science, you understand: No plumbing of depths, just putting in order the things that you see, A and B, A and B.

Now, you may ask, what has this to do with the law? Well think about it. The classical Roman lawyers were scientists in the style of Newton. Old Gaius, Papinian, and Ulpian in ancient Rome went about their work, as they thought, in a scientific manner. They looked at legal cases and such-like and delved below the surface looking for the deeper principles and policies that explained the decisions. The cases and decisions were, so to speak, the surface ripples. The policies and principles were the deep currents that lay beneath and controlled them. They were always beating that into their students. "Never mind the rules and the decisions", they would say, "get to the reasons, *ratio enim anima legis*[33] and all that". And they made their students learn a couple of thousand Latin maxims every day, such as *de minimis non curat lex*.[34] But now, Mr. Austin comes along, and sez he:

"Ulpian, you've got it all wrong; that's no way to do science."

"Quid?" sez Ulpian.[35]

"I mean you're at that plumbin' the depths stuff instead of the A's and B's."

"Pro quo," sez Ulpian.

---

[33] "Reason is the very soul of the law*. The maxim continues *' mutatione legis ratione mutatur et lex* (as the reason changes so does the law).

[34] The law does not concern itself with trifles.

[35] O'Flynn's Latin is no better than his German.

"It's all very simple, you do it just like Mr. Newton would have done it if he'd listened to me. You just look at the laws, decide which A is followed by which B and ignore the maxims."

"Quomodo?" sez Ulpian.

"Easy," sez Austin, "the law consists of commands, and the As and the Bs are just the two parts of a command. For example, I may say to you that if you do (or don't do) A, I am going to hand you B (a punishment)."

"Sed," sez Ulpian, "quo vadis ratio"[36].

"Not needed," sez Austin, "if you have your commands and your threats down pat, nobody will ask you for reasons."

"Et jurisconsultus leges utrum bonos an malum non considerat?"[37]

"No, that's the job of a different science - legislation. You learn that in the Department of Legislation in the School of Ethics down the road."

So Austin found the lawyers trying to be deep thinkers and moralists and so on, and he told them they were all wrong. Their business is to describe the law as it is. Tidy it up a bit, shorten it down a lot, and never mind whether it's good or bad; that's somebody else's job.

So Austin's new legal scientists will look over a pile of statutes and cases lyin' all over the place, put them in order, and maybe summarize them into a book. You might think that this was a job for the janitor or the housemaid, but let's be fair. You had to think about it once in a while. For instance, a statute might say, "No bars to open before the weekend," and a judge on the other hand might decide that it was all right to drink on Wednesday. So one legal analyst might say to another.[38]

"Mick, we've got a problem here."

---

[36] What happened to reason.

[37] Lawyers don't need to bother with reasons.

[38] I'm afraid so – another fictional conversation.

"Not at all, Phelim," sez Mick, "no problem."

"No problem, Mick?"

"None whatsoever, we just say that the weekend starts on Wednesday."

[tumultuous cheers]

This is what you might call a harmonization, and, as you can see, it comes very near to legislation (which we're not supposed to do). I'll come back to that later, if I remember.[39]

Now Austin changed the meaning of another old legal expression, namely the *ratio decidendi*. This used to mean the reasons for the court's decisions, such as that the defendant was a bad man or that the courts had always decided such cases in a particular way in the past and so on and so forth: but not any more. Austin goes up to the judge and sez he:

"Yer honor, do you make the law or just apply it?"

Sez the judge **[looking nervously over his shoulder]** "Who's askin'?"

"You don't need to worry about that any more," says Austin, "from now on you will be making the law freely and openly in your court. You can legislate all you want."

Judge **[beaming]** "I can?"

"Certainly," sez Austin, "we're going to let you pronounce the *ratio decidendi* in each and every case."

"I seem to have heard of that somewhere," says the judge, "but just refresh my memory a bit."

"You can forget anything you heard about it before" says Austin "because it's going to be quite different now."

---

[39] He didn't.

"Oh?" sez the judge.

"Yes" says Austin "it used to be just the reasons for your decision: but not any more. You remember I told you could make all the law you like. Well I'm afraid that's not quite true."

"I might have known" sez the judge.

"Right" sez Austin "You're only allowed to make just enough law to decide the case. If you make too much - go too wide, so to speak - the extra bit is not binding, as we say, but only *obiter dictum*.[40] But the little bit that is just the right size to decide the case will be the *ratio decidendi*."

"Very good," sez the judge, "but how will I know when I'm too wide."

"You won't", sez Austin.

"Could I not just ask somebody?" sez the judge.

"Oh! yes indeed – and all sorts of people will tell you", says Austin, "the next court your case is cited in, some law writer, in fact, just about anybody but yourself will know what the *ratio dicidendi* is."

[At this point a student falls of his chair]

Wonderful! O'Byrne has succumbed already and I haven't told you a quarter of it yet. There's at least a half million definitions - what law is, what's a command, who is the sovereign, what are rights, duties and privileges. If I went into it all, I'd be talking to your children and grandchildren. So you may wonder how a real sleeper like Austin could change the world. But as I've told you, never underestimate an obscure writer, even if he is dull and boring too.

But that brings me to my next question. How did his book do? The answer is very well indeed. You may wonder how? and the answer is, by

---

[40] A remark by the judge not required to decide the question and which can therefore be ignored

luck; but not just ordinary luck; it's more like being lucky enough to be in the right place at the right time. Mr. Marx is a good example. He was even duller and more boring than Austin. But around that time some fellows were thinking of starting a revolution to deliver the poor and oppressed and they got hold of his book. They didn't understand a word of it of course but they liked one or two of his phrases, like "workers unite" and " to each according to his need and from each according to his ability." Before you know it Marx was famous. His book was a best seller and he was rich. If he had got any richer he would have started oppressing the poor himself. Well, it was the same with Austin. He said the right things to the right people at the right time, and that's all it takes. His book coincided nicely with a move by the leading lawyers to improve legal education. The laws were getting reformed all over the place, and they got to thinking that they should improve the lawyers while they were at it. So somebody, the Lord Chancellor maybe, went to the Queen and sez he:

"Yer majesty, we have to get these young law students out of the Inns of Court, for they're learnin' very little law and a lot of bad habits."

"Where will we put them?" sez she.

"Where else," sez he, "but in the University."

"But," sez she, "in the University they're all scientists now".

"No matter, yer majesty," sez he, "we'll teach the law scientifically and I have the very book that'll do it."

"You have?" sez she.

"I have," sez he [pullin' Austin out of his pocket]. Would you like to read it?"

"No, thank you," sez she [weighin' it in her hand], but you go right ahead and do it.

[And he did]

So every young student had to buy the book and read it. A student in America, Christopher Columbus Langdell, bought it - and read it! He was most impressed. He wanted to make the study of law scientific too and he thought Austin's book was just the ticket for the job. Eventually they made him Dean of the Harvard Law School and Austin was off to the races again. Law students on both sides of the pond[41] were reading his book now. As time went by, some of them were bound to become judges and chancellors and such; and they made sure that all the young up and coming lawyers would have to read it and suffer as they had suffered. Austin, who was dead by this time, had it made.

What issued from Austin's success? Now we are getting to the heart of the paternity question. I will list the good and the bad in order.

First the good, such as there is of it:

English law got a little much needed order.

Statutes and regulations and cases were littered all over the place. Austin's boys got them all neatly stacked away in the right boxes. They summarized the law into rules and put the rules into books. It got a lot more consistent and a lot easier to find. So far so good!

Another good thing was that the judges got to be a lot more careful about what they said and what the reporters wrote down. In fact, they got so nervous that they started handing written opinions to the reporters so as to take no chances[42] (it's a big responsibility to be producing "*ratio decidendis*" every day); and lawyers were soon busy reading up on these opinions looking for the *ratio decidendis*. So everybody was paying more attention to their work which was a good thing, especially for the people that publish law reports.

Finally, Austin helped to get the teaching of law into the Universities, which provided good jobs for learned lawyers. And these learned lawyers passed along some of their learning to their grateful students - ahem!

[Cheers - someone takes the hint and refills his glass]

---

[41] I.e. the Atlantic Ocean

[42] This had already happened centuries before Austin.

Thank you. Now to the debit side.

Austin set out to make the study of the law "scientific." Lawyers were to analyze their materials and produce rules of law just like the "if A then B" things we mentioned earlier. The law is to be seen as a set of terse commands. And these commands needed no reasons, at least not so far as lawyers are concerned.

A judge might say "there's a statute here that's dead against you, counsellor".

"But yer honor," sez the lawyer, "I want to draw the attention of the court to the purposes and policies behind that particular statute."

"You will do no such thing," sez the judge

[puffin' out his well worn copy of Austin].

"Us lawyers has no business with morals and purposes."

Now this makes no sense at all and I will prove it to you with one clear example. We have a law which prohibits the Red Cross from buying blood from donors. "Good enough", you say. But wait! You can't pay for the blood with money, but are you allowed to give the donor his cab fare to the clinic or buy him a drink afterwards or even give him a cookie to nibble on? How do you define payment? If the reason for the rule is included as part of the law, there is no problem. For example, the purpose of the rule is probably to prevent sailors from selling their blood, for sailors will lie about their malaria and dear knows what else they have to get the price of a drink. But what sailor in his right mind would tell lies about his diseases just to get a cookie or a ride in a taxi to some place where he can get a needle stuck in his arm. We might, however, be wise to draw the line short of giving them money, for sailors like anybody else can get desperately thirsty. Ahem!

[Someone again takes the hint and fills his glass]

Thank you.

So the laws and the reasons for the laws are part and parcel of the same thing; like man and wife[43] or text and context, they can't and shouldn't be separated from one another.

The next bad thing Austin left us was a change in the meaning of the phrase *ratio decidendi* itself. Austin's method of handling case law is a nightmare We are asked to search in each case for the ratio decidendi and told furthermore that it is "the proposition of law required to decide the case." But what is it? and where is it? The *ratio decidendi* is usually described[44] as the most restricted and narrow rule or rules of law implied in and necessary to make the decision[45]; but implied by whom and necessary according to whom? Not the judge! If he was to stand on his head and swear that the next words he uttered would be the *ratio decidendi*, it wouldn't make a bit of difference. A later court could just as easily decide that what he said was *obiter dictum*; and the court after that could reverse the second court and say that what they had said was obiter and the first judge was correct and so *ad infinitum*.[46] Where, I ask you, is the scientific certainty of the law that Austin was looking for?

The old meaning of the *ratio decidendi*, the reasons used by the court to reach the decision,[47] was better. It was certainly plainer. When the lawyers before Austin read cases they looked for the rules of law, or crucial facts or policies or moral notions, in fact the things that made the court decide the case one way rather than another. Sometimes it was a hard task to find these things, but Austin made it impossible, not to say ridiculous.

Finally, and worst of all, Austin directed the attention of lawyers away from human values; ideals about man and nature; opinions and views on society; and generally those lofty notions that fire the imagination and inspire the souls of humankind, even if they happen to be lawyers. And thus bereft of the heart and soul of the business, lawyering properly so called died and lawyers became logical plumbers. No offense intended to any plumbers present. I have nothing but admiration for plumbers unless

---

[43] No doubt another addendum by Mrs. O"Houlihan?
[44] By the early Austinians.
[45] Good radical empirical epistemology.
[46] As happened in the case of Goss v. G., P. p.15 (1948); See Note, 64 Law Quarterly Review, p.615.
[47] I don't think that lawyers ever described the *ratio decidendi* in such liberal terms

they are pretending to be lawyers as well. Now there were mechanical lawyers before Austin, but Austin made it respectable. In the name of philosophy Austin wooed us away from true philosophy, from the love of wisdom and appreciation of the values and principles that have nourished and given life to the law in all the creative periods of its history.

[all in tears - some alcoholic, some genuine]

I charge you then, ladies and gentlemen of the jury, that if you shall find, as the facts clearly show, that John Austin was around at the right time and that his activities have produced generations of so-called lawyers, hired champions who offer trial by battle, hacking at one another with mindless rules and precedents, lacking the deep understanding of the law that a properly educated lawyer ought to have, then you have no alternative but to find that he is indeed the father of our jurisprudence and he should be ashamed of himself.

At this point a bespectacled young woman identifying herself as Miss Philomena McMurtagh, a biology student, rose and asked whether the law was like human beings and could only have one father or whether, like a litter of kittens, there could be several. On the latter supposition, she said, John Austin might be regarded as the dominant genetic influence, the ginger tom from next door, so to speak, but other parents might have contributed something also, i.e., a person or persons unknown might be included in the verdict.

[O'Houlihan, ever the perfect gentleman, responded courteously]

Ahem! A very interesting point my dear. But time is pressing and I suggest that we consider this the question at bar and address it to the curate [48]in the next room.

**[Thunderous applause. Meeting adjourned
for discussion in the proper spirit]**

---

[48] A euphemism for the bar tender, considered in Irish pubs to be the final arbiter on all questions whatsoever.

COMMENT

1. O'Houlihan's negative assessment of John Austin is still widely held. John Austin's reputation as a legal philosopher has gone through several phases. After his death his reputation soared and he was practically worshipped. On the rare occasion when someone differed from him it was with some remark such as "far be it from me to differ from Mr. Austin---." It was during this phase that he was termed "the father of English jurisprudence." Later, however, especially following the second world war, criticism mounted, directed at his "legal positivism" that is that law should be interpreted and applied without considering whether it was good or bad. The problem here was brought to the attention of lawyers by the events of the Nuremberg trials. The defense of the Nazi officials charged with war crimes was that they were simply obeying the law of Germany in place at that time. Prosecutors were then compelled to argue that there was a higher moral law that was to be followed when the law of the jurisdiction was clearly bad[49]. Lon Fuller of Harvard early voiced this criticism and was later followed by Ronald Dworkin who criticized Austin and HLA Hart, together as legal positivists.

2. The present fiction sits squarely in the second very critical group, who see Austin's descriptive jurisprudence as a purely factual approach to law with all moral considerations omitted entirely. O'Houlihan hammers home this criticism, accusing Austin of stripping the law of all the great values and principles that have been its life blood. In short he stands with law in its older forms, deriving from and resting on general principles which are basically moral or at least value driven in character. These, he says, have been eradicated from the law by Austin leaving the legal profession without ideals or any behavioral standards, like plumbers as he puts it. The law now consists of sovereign commands to be obeyed without questioning.

3. How far is this criticism valid?; only partially. Austin clearly states that a wicked law should not be obeyed. If necessary the judge or other legal officer should resign their post in protest. And he did not

---

[49] Austin of course would have fully agreed with them.

plan to remove values from law in general. He only wished to keep law improvement questions out of legal science. He wanted legal science to be like the positive sciences, especially the then current favorite chemistry, where moral evaluation was irrelevant. We do not consider the various configurations of carbon compounds good or bad, they are just the way they are. And the morality of the behavior of animals is similar. We describe them, we do not consider whether they are good or bad.[50] Similarly he thought that jurisprudence, the science of law, should describe the structure of the law and how it applies in human society as it currently is, without considering how it might be improved. But this does not necessarily mean that moral values and principles already in the law can be ignored. They have a function there. Austin (and Hart and current writers in the Austinian camp) calls this descriptive jurisprudence. But they err in saying that moral values only come into play when we are creating new law or considering law reform. This Austin, following Bentham, appertains to a different science, the science of legislation. Values critical of the law can only be involved in the practice of law when a change in the law is being considered, and the court is authorized to change it. This in Bentham's and Austin's terms is described as judicial legislation.[51] This idea, that values only come into play when a change in the law is being considered, is not uncommon. Roy L Stone in his article *The Compleat Wrngler* [52]argues that once a precedent is established as law, the reasons for its adoption become irrelevant. Hart says much the same thing. But is this really so? Are they not always implicitly present even when e.g. in simple cases, we do not bother to bring them into the picture. If someone beats me over the head with a baseball bat, without an excuse (such as self defense) we treat it as a battery and do not bother to go over the purposes of the law. But they are there all the same, even if we only expressly consider them in difficult or unusual cases when we must resort to them in order to interpret and apply the law. Battery

---

[50] Some biologists characterize the behavior of an occasional monkey or porpoise as"bad".

[51] Bentham hated judicial legislation, but Austin thoroughly approved of it, saying the law would be in a terrible mess if the courts had not stepped in and revised it now and then.

[52] 30 Minn LR 1960

is defined as an unexcused harmful or offensive touching, but what is a touching? Commonly there is no doubt as to whether or not I have been touched. But in an unusual case we may have to step back and consider the purposes of the law of battery i.e. to prevent harmful or offensive touching. So when a bookstore manager forcibly pulled a book from the hand of someone he mistakenly thought was shop lifting, this was declared a touching and therefore a battery since the action was insulting. In a later case the plaintiff, fleeing from a pursuer; got into his car and locked the doors and windows. The pursuer went round the car kicking the tires and this was ruled to be a battery on the basis of the bookstore case, which was read as holding that touching something that I am touching is a "touching" for the purposes of battery. But in an odd kind of case like this one, the purposes of battery should have been considered, and since the defendant's actions were neither harmful or insulting, the offense should not have been held to be a battery. Also since there was no immediate danger of physical harm, it was not an assault. It was not even trespass to goods as there was no damage to the tires. It might well have been some statutory criminal offense but not a civil one.

4. The above considerations are in line with a major linguistic logic principle that language can only properly be meaningful if we consider the intent of the writer or speaker, or to put this in legal terms, "no rules without reasons". In the description of legal rules it is therefore always important to have in mind the reasons for the rules. In medieval times right up almost to the present, this principle was kept alive by reference to legal maxims, little pithy sayings usually in Latin, occasionally in Norman French or in one or two cases in Anglo-Saxon. They were used to guide the application of the law in individual cases[53]. The medieval lawyers thought that the maxims were principles of Natural Law, which is very unlikely, they are too particular for a start. What they probably represent is more detailed aims and objectives of laws as they are applied in particular cases. And these detailed aims and objectives are not derived by logical progression from the maxims. They arise independently of

---

[53] *Qui peccat ebrius luat sobrius* (Injure drunk pay sober) is a nice example.

the maxims although they are justified by them. From this point of view they underline how important it is in any area of law to articulate clearly the purposes and values which that branch of the law serves. Austin, Hart, Stone and many others have missed this important point. Law, unlike Chemistry, is goal directed and the goals must be clearly included in the description.

5. Let us now consider the main question taken up in the O'Houlihan fiction, namely whether Austin was or was not the father of English Jurisprudence. The current thinking on the part of Austin's supporters is to modify his definitions (replace them indeed) to bring them in line with more recent thought. This has been carried out so radically as to make one wonder if there is anything left of Austin's original positions. Austin's sovereign commands are now replaced by "generally accepted rules" His "sovereign" is no longer a person or group of persons but the constitutional system. The simple analysis of laws into "requests with the threat of punishment", has also been replaced to allow the possibility of complex arrangements in legal theory (though with little or no suggestion as to how this might be achieved). So what remains? Two things. First he took the methodology of the physical sciences, especially chemistry and applied it to law, thus making law a descriptive science. Second he presented legal science as the organizing of technical terms, foreseeing in part the idea of game theory using technical terms as the pieces.

6. Clearly his work is a watershed dividing the law previous to his time from that which came later. Until Austin, law was written and taught in medieval and classical terms, arranged with a vertical logic, i.e. with the particular cases seen as logically deriving from and following down from general principles (maxims), Savigny, a contemporary of Austin, considered this to be the scientific way to organize and practice law. Austin introduced a horizontal logic, adapting the descriptive model of the physical sciences for legal purposes. So he took "science" generally to be the organizing of data, and "legal science" to be the organizing of verbally defined technical terms, which can be applied to dispute situations. They did not come down from heaven they were produced here below.

The great Victorian law books which followed Austin did just that. They presented the law apparently as rules, but in effect as technical terms which they defined verbally and showed how they had been applied in case law. This was an enormous advance on anything that had gone before, and these works were well adapted to the needs of practicing lawyers. The worth of this approach can be appreciated when we consider how many editions these great books went through before they were finally replaced. And their replacements generally followed much the same method.

7.   But something more remains to be done to bring the science of law into line with current models of science. Neither Austin nor his critics have been able to supply a satisfactory method for a science of law. Modern science has gone way beyond description in any ordinary meaning of that word. The universe is described in terms of complex mathematical models. Law likewise needs a more complex descriptive method. It is not enough to say that we are simply describing it A complex model of legal science will be presented in the later fictions, "Underside" and especially in "The Ballet of the Books"

PART THREE

THE BISINESS OF THE LAW –PREDICTION

An introduction to American Legal Realism

THE AUTHORS

Stanley Hammerberg and Richard Rodgerstein

Hammerberg and Rodgerstein in concert

Stanley Hammerberg is loosely based on a former assistant law librarian at Campbell, now alas! out there practicing law. He was invariably helpful to students with an uncanny ability to dig up obscure references and was also an indefatigable jogger; in fact there was nothing against his character until now except the occasional Groucho Marx imitation. The charge that he wrote this script may of course be false.

His collaborator, Richard Rodgerstein, based on our one time computer expert, wrote the music, fortunately not included in the text. He also built the computers for the set and insisted on absolute realism; they computed and also exploded at the first performance. A number of people are looking for him and there is a small reward for any information as to his whereabouts.

Morgan La Fey demonstrating her magic boxes

CAMPBELLOT

An Unmusical Based on the Tale
"King Arthur and the Magic Boxes"
adapted by
Stanley Hammerberg and Richard Rodgerstein
(who also sang the parts of Arthur and Merlin)

Dramatis Personae

Merlin (Richard Rodgerstein)
Arthur (Stanley Hammer)
Mordred
Morgan le Fey
Clerk
Sir Lancelot du Lac
Lunkhead, a peasant
Thicky, another peasant

ACT I

SCENE. - The Royal Castle of the Angles and Saxons

Merlin: [*Enters singing*]

I wonder why the king's so dreary at night
Whatever makes the king so weary at night
Why is it that his back's so stooped
Why ever are his ears so drooped.

Arthur. [*Enters staggering*] He's pooped.

Merlin. Why so tired, your majesty?

Arthur. I'm not just tired, I'm exhausted. I've been in the Witan[54] every day dealing with lawsuits, land titles, marital disputes, punch-ups - I've had it I tell you.

[*He sings*]

They comealot
They comealot
Each wronged and injured Briton
Comes running to the Witan
There's scarcely a moment when the Witan Isn't sittin'.

[He throws out his arms melodramatically to Merlin.]

What shall I do? Could you not use your magic to settle some of these lawsuits and give me a break?

Merlin. Now then, wart, you know I taught you not to rely on magic but on reason. It's time for one of your philosophical soliloquies - you know, "Proposition, etc.

---

[54] The court of the Anglo-Sxons

Arthur. Oh! yes. [**He poses.**] Proposition! The king is the fountain of justice and so should be available to try every difficult case; but if I hear both sides carefully and think about the matter properly, I'll have no time to rule or to rest. How to reconcile these two contrary interests?

[Light of intelligence springs into his eye.]

I've got it!

Merlin. What is it?

Arthur. I'll get my clerks to write out brief descriptions of the relevant facts in the usual disputes that come before us. It shouldn't be hard to do; all cases boil down to a few standard types.

Merlin. Yes? and?--

Arthur. Well, anyone who wants to bring a case to the Witan will have to go to my clerks and pick out one of these forms, fill in his name and one or two other details and behold, the case is ready for trial. We can try it by putting the hot iron on his hand, ducking him in the pond, or we might order an inquest to decide the truth of the matter. I tell you, Merlin, this will save so much time that I'll be home early for supper every night.

[He bursts into song again. Merlin winces because Stanley's tenor is even worse than Richard's baritone.]

Won't say a lot
But they'll pay a lot
One who has been disseized from his fee farms
Won't talk all day of injuries and harms
He'll simply bring trespass with force and arms[55]
There won't be any trial by battles

---

[55] Trespass vi et armis was centuries away - but who cares?

Just trespass to chattles[56]

Merlin. Wonderful!

Arthur. Wait, there's more.

Merlin. I was afraid of that.

Arthur. When these "forms of action" are well known
We'll give each one a number of its own
Replevin could be seven
And number fifty two be detinue.
Then we really will be saving time.

Merlin. What ghastly rhyme!

Arthur. Well, Merlin what do you think?

Merlin. It certainly seems more promising than that round table thing you came up with yesterday. But I seem to remember something bad about it in the future.

[Mordred has been eavesdropping]

Mordred. You can count on that. I'll see to it. I'll go to my aunt Morgan la Fey in the woods and enlist her help.

SCENE. - The Enchanted Wood.

Mordred. [Shouting] Morgan, Morgan le Fey, dear aunt, help me, and I will give you a wagonload of chocolates.

Morgan le Fey. How is it that I can conjure up invisible castles and all that, and yet I can't produce chocolates?

---

[56] Presumably the writ of *trespass de bonis asportatis* (trespss to goods) also centuries ahead of its ime.

Mordred. Because it would ruin the plot of this musical for a start. Now aunt, Arthur is going to revolutionize the law business by providing a specific writ for each type of injury. He thinks it will make him famous. How can we spoil it for him?

[Leers horribly, strikes a match on his crutch and spits.]

Morgan le Fey. What did you have in mind?

Mordred. A paper shortage perhaps?

Morgan le Fey. No, you fool, eventually this scheme will not require paper.

Mordred. So what can we do?

Morgan le Fey. Help him, of course. My instincts tell me that this thing will get out of hand and everybody will curse the invention, including the inventor.

Mordred. How will you do this?

Morgan le Fey. I'll build a machine for Arthur - a magical box, a law machine. There will be no need for a court. You pick up your writ, put it in the slot and out comes the verdict. So Arthur doesn't have to go to court. He just has to be king and make the laws to put in the box.

Mordred. And that's bad?

Morgan le Fey. Yes.

Mordred. I don't see how.

Morgan le Fey. Of course you don't, you fool. You must wait and see.

ACT II

SCENE. - The Witan. All members of the Witan (or wits, as they were called in Anglo-Saxon) are standing round looking at a large black box sitting beside Arthur's throne.

Arthur. Morgan, are you sure this will work?

Morgan le Fey. I'm positive.

Arthur. If it does, it will relieve all doomsmen from the burden of court service, and me of the trouble of waiting for them to make up their minds. If it is successful, I will reward you handsomely.

Morgan le Fey. With chocolates?

[She has obviously put on a few pounds since her last appearance.]

Arthur. If that's what you want. Now to the demonstration. First case, please.

Clerk. "The Fresh Air of Campbellot v. Sir Lancelot du Lac."

[Enter Lancelot surrounded by hostile knights.]

Clerk. Gentlemen, state your complaint against Sir Lancelot?

Sir Galahad. He has polluted the pure air of Campbellot with his constant bragging, boasting and sermonizing. It was heavenly round here before he came; now, it is

Clerk. [To Arthur.] Sounds like No. 66 "infernal nuisance," your Majesty.

Arthur. Pop it in.

**[He does. Wheezing, flashing lights, and a
bell; card pops out; clerk picks it up.]**

Clerk. [Reads.] "Not to see Queen Guinevere for a month".

Arthur. [Experiencing a glimmering of insight.] What! What's that?

Sir Lancelot. [A resourceful fellow] I shall miss those literary and theological conversations with the Queen, your Majesty.

Arthur. [Glimmer fading.] Quite! Next case.

[Enter two peasants pulling on a cow from opposite ends.]

Lunkhead. [Pulling on the horns] He stole my cow.

Thicky. [Pulling on the tail.] Nay, your Majesty, I found it.

Arthur. Number forty two, Trover, would you agree?

Clerk. Right, your Majesty.

[Pops in card number forty two - print-out emerges - Clerk reads.]

Conversion - Thicky to buy Lunkhead's cow at the going rate.

Arthur. [To Morgan le Fey.] Wonderful, Morgan, you have earned a wagon load of chocolates. I won't have to sit here every day deciding cases. I can use the time with my thanes in devising new laws and new writs to ensure that we keep up with changing circumstances and recent thought. Could you have these new writs incorporated into the machine?

Morgan le Fey. Certainly, but I can do better than that.

[Winks conspiratorially at Mordred.]

Mordred. [In a hoarse whisper.] What are you up to?

Morgan le Fey. It'll cost you another wagon load of chocolates.

Mordred. Done!

Morgan le Fey. [**To Arthur.**] Arthur, I can save you and the Witan even more trouble.

Arthur. How?

Morgan le Fey. I have here, concealed under this cloth, a second machine which makes new laws as they become necessary.

[She whips the cover of a second even larger magic box]

Arthur. Impossible! Laws must be made with careful thought. Changing circumstances must be noted and evaluated, competing values weighed, compromises made, consequences foreseen; finally, the various solutions must be compared and one selected which provides that optimum balance between all the competing elements, that harmony in fact which we call justice.

Morgan le Fey. You're sure?

Arthur. I am certain. All my instruction in Jurisprudence by a devout Hibernian[57] has led me irrevocably to these conclusions.

Morgan le Fey. Well, think again. These values of which you speak, are they changing and transient or are they immutable and eternal?

Arthur. The latter, of course.

Morgan le Fey. Could one represent them in writing or by symbols and assign relative weights to them by numbers?

Arthur. Conceivably.

---

[57] Who might that be?

Morgan le Fey. Could one not then put such systems into the machine?

Arthur. I suppose so.

Morgan le Fey. And the changing circumstances that you mention, where would you and the Witan find them?

Arthur. Inscribed in the Saxon Daily Chronicle, of course.

Morgan le Fey. And the various legal possibilities, where would you find those?

Arthur. In the Campbellot Law Review, naturally.

Morgan le Fey. And could not any neophyte in the law select these and put them into the machine?

Arthur. Perhaps.

Morgan le Fey. And how would you decide which of the possible solutions was the best?

Arthur. Well, I could try to imagine their future effects, and I might ask around a few folks to see how they would like them; and I might also pray or ask Merlin.

Morgan le Fey. Do you really think you are the best qualified person to do all this?

Arthur. Well, I have studied long in the liberal arts.

Morgan le Fey. What about the social sciences?

Arthur. Why no!

Morgan le Fey. Well, what sort of person do you think would be best qualified to say if a proposed measure was of a type which worked effectively in the past or was likely to work well in the future?

Arthur. I suppose one who was skilled in the calculation of probabilities.

Morgan le Fey. Good, and?

Arthur. Who could select a relatively small number of persons for a trial in such a way that they would effectively represent the whole population?

Morgan le Fey. Yes, and ?

Arthur. Perhaps one who was skilled in studying complex social conditions to perceive and isolate causes and effects.

Morgan le Fey. Correct! and you have just described what sort of person?

Arthur. [*Hopefully.*] Not the king?

[Laughter.]

Morgan le Fey. [Emphatically] Certainly not.

Arthur. You don't mean - a soc-man.[58]

Morgan le Fey. Who else?

Arthur. So you are telling me that I do not even need to make the laws any more. Teams of soc-men will gather the appropriate statements from various sources and feed them into this second box which will, if necessary, invent a new remedy.

Morgan le Fey. You are baking the cakes over a hot fire?[59]

---

[58] Strictly speaking this means one holding land in a non-military tenure. Here I think the author is indicating a sociologist!!

[59] I think this is meant to represent "now you are cooking with gas.

Arthur. Could I have a demonstration?

Morgan le Fey. Certainly, and I have a case for you. It seems to me that I have spent a lot of time producing this machine to save you work and that you owe me another wagonload of chocolate.

Arthur. But I don't recall any agreement, and there was certainly no covenant.

Morgan le Fey. True, but there was *quid pro quo* [60] and I think it's time we fed all this into the box. I have it here.

[Puts cards in the slot - whirring lights, grinding noises, a bell - a card drops out.]

Arthur. [Reads it.] Unjust enrichment? What does this mean?

Morgan le Fey. It means another wagonload of chocolates, for a start.

Arthur. Oh, very well. I suppose it's worth it, although all that is left for me to do now is to come to the court once in a while and pick up the money that people have paid into the boxes.

Morgan le Fey. Wrong.

Arthur. Wrong?

Morgan le Fey. Right! These boxes aren't going to be in the courtroom. Mordred and I are opening a hyper-agora [61] across the road and are putting these boxes in there. We're calling the store Roebuck-Seers. Nobody will be needing kings or lawyers any more. Such and such a length, lamprey! [62]

Mordred. Two wagonloads of chocolate for this, aunt.

---

[60] An element in the later equitable form of contract'
[61] I think this is supposed e mean a supermarket
[62] A lamprey is a parasitic fish which attaches itself to its victim by sucker i.e. "so long sucker"

Arthur. *Wait.* I see it all now. These are devilish devices. No machine could possibly deliberate wisely and act justly like a rational being.

**[He calls Lancelot, who had been moping in the corner.
He jumps up and comes over to the King.]**

Arthur. Lancelot, these machines are going to destroy the law.

Lancelot. But I respect, I love the law.

Arthur. Yes, and remember the stiff sentence the machine gave you. Take Excalibur and charge them. You alone are brave enough - and stupid enough - to do it.

[He intends him to charge Morgan le Fey and Mordred.]

Sir Lancelot. [Sings in Norman-French, worse than Merlin or even Arthur.]

C'est Moi, C'est Moi
J'aime beaucoup la loi.
Aussi je deteste les machines
I Lancelot du Lac
Les donnez le whack
Le thump et le crack
Les jamais[63] no more will be seen
Then back to the Queen.

[Sir Lancelot, misunderstanding Arthur's admittedly ambiguous orders, believes that he is to attack the machines rather than Mordred and Morgan le Fey. He charges, hacking the boxes, cutting all the cables and thrusting his sword into every available slot and opening. Sparks, crackling noises, and explosions. Parts begin to fly out. Morgan le Fey rushes to protect her property. She seizes excalibur out of Lancelot's hand but some sparks get into her eyes and blind

---

[63] The Norman French expires here.

her. There is a mighty explosion, and the machines disintegrate into fragments. A pair of scales - probably those used in the machine to balance values and interests against one another - fly out and land in her outstretched hand. Morgan le Fey stands stunned and blinded. This is probably the prototype for the statue of the goddess of justice that has graced our courthouses ever since.]

Finis

COMMENT

1. This fiction is obviously intended to represent American Legal Realism, a movement designed to update and modernize American law, which the Realists considered so far behind the times that it was like someone sitting in the stadium when the game was being played somewhere else

2. The obvious question here is what constitutes the modernity that the realists sought to introduce into the law. They identified a number of new trends of which the law should take notice and redesign itself accordingly. These were:
   (i)   Freudian analytic psychology
   (ii) Marxism
   (iii) Radical empiricist epistemology
   (iv) Social science
   (v)   Some would add Darwinian optimism as a fifth factor which was not explicitly advocated by the realists, but was exemplified in the bold confidence with which they promoted their radical proposals. "Fortune favors the bold".

All these trends were already present in the latter years of the nineteenth century, but they were not taken seriously until after the second world war, which shook up society and culture to such an extent that people were more ready to listen to new ideas and consider running with them

3. It is difficult to imagine the influence that Freud's ideas exercised in the years after the second world war. They permeated the lives of even high school students who were fascinated by the idea that our conscious thinking was driven and controlled by powerful unconscious forces, especially sex. Before Freud, thinking was persuasive. After Freud it was revealing, making public the workings of our subconscious and unconscious mind. One of Freud's ideas which was immediately deemed relevant to law, was his notion of *rationalization* where the mind put forward as rational thinking what was really much less presentable processing, the product of unconscious or subconscious forces. The result was suspicion by the realists of the reasoning found in judicial opinions and legal briefs, and trying to get behind them to see what were the real reasons behind the arguments. What this boiled down to was a different reading of case law, ignoring the judicial reasoning and looking for *operative facts*, the facts (of any kind whatever) that actually influenced the court to decide the case one way or the other[64]

4. Radical empiricism was then very much in the ascendant in the twenties and thirties. Investigators were encouraged to stick closely to the facts and keep theory, which was viewed as speculative and uncertain, to the bare minimum, Herman Oliphant's new science of case law was explicitly developed along these lines, identifying the operative facts in cases and organizing them into numerous small groups (boxes) all of which had been decided in the same way. All that practicing lawyers had to do then was fit the facts of their cases into the most appropriate box and then you had the most probable legal outcome. But identifying the small groups of cases and allocating them to an appropriate box was no easy task for the legal scientist, and I am not sure what progress, if any, was made along these lines. One major problem was the way in which these operative facts were viewed. They were not only the facts of the case as presented in the court record. but also any external facts that may have operated clandestinely in the decision. e.g. that one of the parties was objectionable in some way or other. Such facts

---

[64] This is more or less the method in Oliphant's new science of case law.

(influences) can be difficult to identify and there could easily be differences of opinion as to whether and what they might be.

5. Social science required the development of statistical mathematics to enable it to make progress. But starting from the work of a rural physician who was trying out various dilutions of his herbal remedies on frogs in his pond, it had come a long way, and had begun to predict social happenings with some success. Indeed it was Underhill Moore's attendance at the meetings of the prestigious Social Science department in Columbia University that sparked off the realist movement. Moore immediately had a vision of how legal theory might be drastically improved if the outcomes of each case could be more accurately predicted. Indeed he and Oliphant and others began to view legal theory as a predictive science. They also hoped that sociological studies might produce accurate and helpful information as to what was really happening in society so that the law might become more relevant to its needs.

6. Marxism was very much in the ascendant in the late twenties and thirties. It appeared to offer a better future for the masses and was much favored by influential intellectuals. Marxists indeed achieved considerable political control of unions and even industries. It was difficult to have a film produced or a book published without the cooperation of Marxist controlled unions.[65] The Marxist theme, as it applied to law, focused on the notion of *ideology*, the ways in which we view ourselves and our contributions to society. Lawyers like to see themselves as knights in shining armor coming to the rescue of the poor and oppressed. According to the Marxists, this is a false ideology. What lawyers are really doing was helping those in power to control the underdogs, by convincing them that they have legal rights and are getting a fair shake. This Marxist theme is missing in Oliphant's manifesto, as it would not have been helpful to his hopes for his realist inaugural address as president of the American Association of Law Schools. It surfaced later in the "critical legal studies" movement which is sometimes described as the last wag of the realists dog's tail.[66]

[65] Ronald Reagan began his political career freeing up the movie industry from Marxist control
[66] A great many critical legal studies writers, but not all, were Marxists.

7. The fiction shows that all of these hopes failed miserably. King Arthur was right when he concluded that the new law machines would be harmful indeed destructive of the law. The Marxist theme especially, dormant at the time, emerged later as he Critical Legal Studies movement which, at least in its more radical forms, would have replaced law altogether with administrative agencies.

8. The saddest part of this whole movement was that it was built on the shifting sands of contemporary culture, which were about to be washed away by radical intellectual and social changes.

    (i)   Freudian psychoanalysis, so pervasive and promising in the twenties and thirties, has been relegated to the back burner and almost pushed off the stove altogether by the current trend in clinical psychology, represented by the Diagnostic and Statistical Manual of Mental Disorders (DSM). This uses statistical methods to develop diagnoses and treatments of psychiatric disorders.

    (ii)   Freud's methods and even his character are currently very critically and even adversely viewed by mainstream psychologists.

    (iii) The Marxist empires, once so dominant and threatening, have either collapsed or reinvented themselves on more or less non-Marxist lines.

    (v)   Radical empiricism is likewise no longer the preferred way to do science. Computer advances have made mathematical errors more or less non existent, even in the massively complex forms used in astrophysics and subatomic studies. Furthermore, excessive caution is no longer the hall mark of good science. Imagination and creativity are currently much more valued.

    (vi)   Even Darwinian optimism has faded drastically since the second world war. It now takes a great deal of faith to be optimistic about the future prospects for any project or even for the human race.

In short there have been drastic social and intellectual changes in our culture, which have rendered much of the realist thinking obsolete.

9. The last matter, which was not raised by the fiction, is the question of the legacy of the American Realist Movement. Few movements which achieve such popularity, however misplaced, leave nothing behind them; and Realism is no exception. The realist movement really began when Roscoe Pound became concerned about the gulf that was developing between commercial practice and the law. He was concerned that large commercial enterprises would opt out of the law altogether and establish their own methods of settling disputes, a thing that has already happened to a considerable extent. This critical concern for the future of the law, communicated to his students, sparked off the realist movement. However, the realists strayed far beyond what Pound was looking for and he dissociated himself from them and criticized them roundly, saying that they had glossed over the vital distinction between legal authorities and influences, which indeed they had. However, on the positive side, the realists have drawn attention to the importance of influences in the courtroom and elsewhere. We cannot cite them in court but we need to be aware that they are there and take what measures we can to avoid their warping the administration of justice.

10. Furthermore the Realists have made us aware not only of the need for lawyers to understand society but also to keep abreast of social developments. Changes in the business environment are evidently important, but we need to keep a weather eye on what is happening in society generally. Finally the realists introduced a number of valuable commercial courses into the law school curriculum.

11. Above all, the Realist movement is a stern warning against being taken in by contemporary fads, including trends and notions and dominant ideas. We are currently more hesitant in our appraisal of cultural trends.

PART FOUR

LIVING FROM MND TO MOUTH

An introduction to logic and the law

**This part is especially about the possible
contributions of linguistic logic to
the study and practice of law.**

OUR AUTHOR

Count Nicolai Dimski
1901 - 1993

The scion of an emigre family who came to England to avoid being eliminated by the secret police of the Czar. The Dimskis did not return to Russia after the revolution since they fancied they would fare no better at the hands of the Bolsheviks. The entire family was talented, and many of them distinguished themselves in the fields of music and literature but especially in mathematics. They were wealthy but devoted themselves completely to their professions on the principle of "noblesse oblige". Count Nicolai published a number of papers, especially on imaginary numbers, but principally interested himself in the mathematician's dream of "squaring the circle". Following his "visit to the underside", he devoted his entire energies to the production of a universal calculus containing every known system of thought in symbolic form. This calculus was designed to eliminate the possibility of linguistic confusion. The count had no hobbies and no interests other than his work. His sole recreation was a short walk every day which he called "circling the square".

UNDERSIDE

A Mathematician's Visit To Hell
by
Count Nicolai Dimski

Count Nicholai Dimski visits the underworld

The following is an account of a dream by the celebrated mathematician, Count Nicolai Dimski. Several psychiatrists have conjectured that the following visions were the result of an obsession which the count developed by brooding on his name (Nick) and age (old), coupled with a fixation on the analogy between his title (count) and his occupation (mathematician). The gentleman in question, however, never doubted the reality of this experience and lived ever afterwards in mortal terror of logical error and linguistic confusion.

I was sitting in my study one afternoon; I remember it was a dull day, when suddenly the light seemed to fail completely and I had the sensation of rushing down a tunnel at incredible speed. I emerged suddenly into a great, brightly lighted room, rather like an enormous airplane hangar. A young man at the nearest desk asked me to state my name and social security number, which I did. He entered them into the computer, stared at the screen for some time in silence and said "there seems to be some error here, we have no reservation for you - unless of course you have merely been pulled down temporarily for briefing?"

"May I ask where I am?" I ventured.

"In Hell, of course," he replied.

"Hell?" I said, "this doesn't look like Hell."

"What did you expect," he replied, "flames and pitchforks? Actually we look and operate just like a large business corporation or a university or the Pentagon - we are a bit like all of them."

"And you are by any chance, the --?"

"Oh dear me, no!" said the young man. "I am not the Devil -merely operator $10^{-11.42}$."

"And where is Old Nick or Mephistopheles or whatever you call him?"

"There is nobody here called Old Nick. We have a Mephistopheles but he isn't the Devil either."

"Well, Satan then."

"Satan is not the Devil; in fact, the Devil is not the Devil. You see all these titles are names assumed by our important diplomats when they go from underside on special missions to earth or Heaven. Mephistopheles, for example, is $10^{-2.1}$ and Satan is $10^{-2.4}$"

"But surely there must be some overall Being in command of all this?"

"Oh, certainly. You are referring to MINUS ONE himself, but we never see Him out here."

"Minus One?"

"Ah yes! our little joke. The opposition thinks He is Number One so we, Hell being the obverse of Heaven, use inverted numbers to identify all our personnel. A nice touch, since we are very logical and mathematical down here."

"Really! I myself am a mathematician."

"Indeed, then you should be able to appreciate us. Mathematics is the name of the game here."

"Excuse me, did you say game?"

"Yes, another nice touch, if I may say so, as we are also very keen on game theory."

"You really surprise me," I said.

"Why should you be surprised? Mathematical games are our business."

"I thought your business was lies."

"In a way, yes, though we prefer to call them alternative viewpoints. But quite frankly we find that kind of thing a bit passé. The growing edge of our business nowadays is linguistic warfare."

"What is that?"

"Well, as a mathematician you are familiar with Boolean logic?"[67]

"Certainly."

"Then you understand that thinking, whether it is done with words or with mental pictures, is really a mathematical process since words or mental images act like the symbols in a mathematical system."

"I have read many of Gottlöb Frege's works, also some Wittgenstein.

"So then the thinking process, since it is mathematical, ought to be certain."

"I suppose so - in theory anyway."

"Ah, but in fact it is not, and I ask you why?"

"Slips and errors in calculation perhaps?"

"Occasionally, but not usually. No, most errors are confusions resulting from mixing one language system with another, slipping unbeknownst from biological language to psychological language or theological language or whatever."

"Yes, I can see that, but how can simple confusions further the purposes of Hell?"

"Why, blast you! [underside for "bless you"] It's our principal weapon. Take the word "cause" for example. By flipping it back and forward from mechanics to biology and psychology we must have made a million influential converts to some form or other of determinism."

---

[67] George Boole was a nineteenth century logician who devised a system of algebraic symbols to represent Aristotelian logic. He did the same thing using numbers. He was born in England but became Professor of Mathematics in the University of Cork in Ireland. An Austrian engineer who became more interested in philosophy, especially he application of game theory to language. He was a major figure in the linguistic language movement.

"Indeed!"

"Ah yes, you would be surprised if you knew how many people think that the same word means the same thing in every language system. Take "proof", for example. Slipping that one around from law to geometry via the science lab has got more of our people out of jail than one of these computers could count in a week".

"But surely such a simple logical error as that would be too obvious, at least for more careful thinkers?"

"You would imagine so, although you might be surprised at the blind spots of the eminent. But consider the more subtle possibilities. Most people are not aware or at least not familiar with the fact that even a small subject or a single conversation may involve several separate systems of thought. It's not too difficult to mix these systems up in peoples' minds, especially if the systems have words in common or are related to one another. Let me show you our computer room so you can see how we do it."

I was instantly transported to a huge room filled with enormous computers in rows, with desk terminals in between, staffed by neatly dressed young men and smartly turned out young women.

"Minus Two is in charge here, which gives you some idea of its importance. Our databases contain every language calculus system that ever was, in every language that ever was, from the most complex right down to little ones with only two words in them."

"You bother with two-word systems?"

"Certainly; one of them -"Mine and Yours" is one of our top lines that keeps people and nations at one another's throats. But to continue - when one of our representatives is working on a case, he contacts our computer room. We look up all the word systems involved and formulate what we call a "declarification plan" for our agent to work with."

"Isn't that a lot of work to go through just for one soul?"

"Well perhaps, but frequently our analyst here is able to recognize a familiar situation and pull out an old plan and use it again. For example, in "porno" cases we just punch in the search command "liberty" and appropriate phrases simply come pouring out. "'Rights" is another word we use a lot. We actually got that one from "Up there". They had it "no rights without duties." We just added that the words should be taken one at a time, rights first, of course. I need hardly tell you our legal computers are very large and very well staffed. We are, however, a little short on mathematicians. Would you by any chance consider coming under board?"

At this point Count Nicolai records that he awakened. Friends pointed out to him that the episode took place shortly after a rather hearty lunch, but he himself never wavered from the view that, by a computer error in Hell, he had been vouchsafed an underview of his own profession from which only a damned fool would fail to profit.

COMMENT

1. This fiction features computers, but it is really concerned with the link between mathematics and reasoning (logic) and the way that these impact on how we think about law. Mathematics has always been at the heart of philosophy, (defined as basic thinking about things). It offers a vision of certainty in a world of mere opinion. When Pythagoras was a young man, wanting to know the truth about things, he visited Thales in Asia minor and that great man (everything is water) advised him to go to Egypt and study mathematics. Plato had the same vision and spent the last years of his life studying mathematics. Descartes too, the great bridge between the middle ages and modernity, looked to the mathematical approach as a way of escape from personal opinions, which he despised, to reach certainty which he considered the mark of truth. The big question here is what is mathematics and what is mathematical method? The

deductive mathematical vision of Pythagoras, Plato and Descartes, led to modern mathematical science and engineering, changing the world. More recently astrophysics and submolecular biology have been developed using very complex mathematics which begin to make our world look like Pythagoras' universe, actually consisting of mathematical stuff..[68] Descartes' has been a good friend to the mathematical sciences and engineering, which were then on the up and up, and they were taken in readily by the burgeoning universities of the time. However, he was not so helpful to other disciplines. The social sciences were, for a time at least, relegated to the philosophy department and only the hard sciences were deemed to be the real thing. Many people continue to think this way. The advent of a new form of mathematics, statistics, offered a way forward for the social sciences, psychology and sociology, which largely operate by statistical method. However, it still gave no hope for disciplines such as law, history, philosophy and theology.

2. A more recent view of the nature of mathematics provides more promise for the non-mathematical disciplines. The most important recent development in the theory of mathematics has been game theory, propounded by a number of late nineteenth century philosophical mathematicians, especially Gottlöb Frege. Frege viewed mathematics as playing games, like chess, where there were pieces (symbols) and moves. In arithmetic the symbols are numbers and the moves such things as addition, subtraction, etc. Algebra is the same except that the symbols were variables, represented by letters. In geometry the symbols are shapes. These games are artificial constructs with no necessary link with reality. They can be made up in your head if you like, in any way you fancy. The only restriction is that the system must be logically consistent throughout. But these formal games can be and usually are applied to practical uses.. Geometry was supposedly developed in Egypt to restore the boundaries of property when the usual landmarks had been washed away by the annual flooding of the Nile. And the devising of mathematical games and their application to practical problems

---

[68] Max Tegmark indeed endorses this idea in "OUR MATHMATICAL UNIVERSE 2014

continues. Statistical mathematics was developed by a family doctor trying to standardize his herbal concoctions to treat heart failure (dropsy). One mathematical madman suggested that mathematics could be based on two numbers ("0" and "1) instead of the usual ten. This remained a curiosity until the development of computers which operate on this very notion, binary mathematics. Another madman developed a game using the mathematical symbol Pi (ϖ), the ratio between the radius and circumference of a circle, (roughly 22/7) instead of 1,2,3 etc. But Pi (π) is known as the natural number because many things in nature are arranged in this way, and this form of mathematics has become very important, especially in the biological sciences. Pure mathematicians are in effect gamesters and many computer games were developed by mathematicians when they arrived home and were playing with their kids.

3. There are many kinds of possible games. The symbols can be iconic diagrams, like the symbols in chemistry (also often represented by letters such as CH4 for carbohydrates). Little pictograms are used by mathematicians to represent several pages of mathematical transformations since inscribing them out in full every time you use them can be tedious.. Little video clips (short stories) are used by historians and lawyers to compare the most likely reading of events. These can be described as "story logics".

4. Frege was aware that game theory could be applied to language, using words as the symbols, and the next move forward in game theory was to apply game theory to language in some detail. For this we are, to a large extent, indebted to Ludwig Wittgenstein, an Austrian engineer turned philosopher, who was a (much younger) friend of Frege. Wittgenstein advanced Frege's idea about language games considerably. He concluded that organized thinking was largely the application of word games for practical purposes. His *Tractatus Mathematico-Philosophicus*, his first and only published book, took the essential function of language to be communication about "things". So the vital clue to the meaning of language was deemed to be how it related to the things we wished to talk about. This led to a very unfruitful brand of philosophy known as *logical positivism*, where the meaning of a word was taken to be the things that you

would point to if anyone doubted that the thing you were talking about existed. As a result any other use of language, where it could not be related to actual things (e.g., philosophy and theology), was not only mistaken, butt consisted of meaningless sounds, like grunts. However, Wittgenstein, after a period of reflection in prison camp following world war II and conversations with friends, eventually realized that there were many other functions of language besides indicating things, such as commands, analogies, jokes, expletives and many more. He therefore expanded the understanding of language to take into account the purposes and objectives of the speaker or writer. If I want to understand what you are saying to me then I must know why you are saying it. A joke cannot be interpreted literally. This way of looking at thinking can be expressed in the simple diagram:

GAME

   PURPOSE

APPLICATION

Diagram representing the place of purposes in applied logics

5. The significance of this view of logical thinking for non mathematical disciplines of every kind is enormous. Science can be redefined in terms that include but go beyond mathematics. Any enterprise using symbols, including words, to arrange things in an orderly manner to achieve defined purposes is scientific. Freudian psychiatry, which Wittgenstein really enjoyed, was, he said, unscientific. But in his own terms he was wrong. Freudian psychiatry uses a raft of well-defined technical terms such as conscious, subconscious and unconscious, neurosis, psychosis etc. and applies them to the diagnosis and treatment of mental disorders. It may not be good science but it is essentially a scientific enterprise.

6. Wittgenstein's redefining science (applying games to things to produce results) opened the door for scientific advances in a number

of non-mathematical disciplines, including Law. I have argued elsewhere[69] that he did not follow through with this aspect of his work, he pointed to the door forward but did not enter through itr himself, largely confining himself to discussing a number of old chestnuts in philosophy that had followed the publishing of the skeptical arguments of David Hume (what do we really see? is knowledge really objective? what is the nature of the self? What kind of an activity is deciding? etc.). But the way forward is clear, we must devise symbolic games suitable to our materials and use them to organize our knowledge in a way that will be useful to us. In law this can be achieved by fitting technical words into algorithms and other games with the terms cross- linked to case law, legislative enactments, administrative regulations,etc.. And the algorithms can be further explained by references to journal articles, and other such materials. Each section must also be supplied with the purposes served by that portion of the law. This is no easy task but it is well worth doing. For further discussion of the application of game theory to legal science see the notes following the *Ballet of the Books* and also Appendix #1 on *Language Logic and the Law*.

---

[69] As yet unpublished paper on Wittgenstein and the law.

THE GOOD AS UTILITY

Jeremy Bentham (1748 – 1832)

Prudential theories of justice

Moral questions are difficult to resolve precisely; and lawyers like to be precise and definite. Sometimes the moral dimension accords well with this propensity and sometimes it does not. When public moral standards are uniform and clearly laid down, there is no problem. But when, as is often the case nowadays, the moral environment is foggy and the landmarks are difficult to discern, it is easy to get lost and feel uncomfortable or at least impatient. Shortcuts which purport to bypass these difficult questions are therefore always popular with lawyers. Two of these are discussed here; Bentham's Utilitarianism and Rawls' contract theory of justice, both of which will be considered, like most shortcuts, to be unsatisfactory.

One way out of the moral dilemma is *legal positivism* - the lawyer is not required to discuss moral questions, only to apply the rules. Some criticism of this view from the formal viewpoint has already been made, as moral maxims seem to operate inside the apparatus of the law so that lawyers are obliged to take notice of them whether they like it or not.

A second alternative is to "translate" moral discussion into more manageable and definite terms by making right and wrong mean "useful" or "likely to produce widespread pleasure" or "general agreement." It is widely assumed that such expedients provide clearer and more definite answers to moral questions than the older philosophical approach. That this assumption can bear a little reflection is the subject of this fiction. A third variant of prudential moral theory to to treat moral values as implied agreements in our decision to cooperate together in a society (social contract theory). This is the approach of John Rawls' THEORY OF JUSTICE. Both of these prudential theories are considered together in the following fiction, Oedipus Lex.

OUR AUTHOR

Diarmuidh ua Dubhne[70] P

A well-known character in the "left bank" area of Dublin. Early in his career he professed to despise formal education, though he had both his bachelors and masters degrees in literature. He had even survived one year in a doctoral program after which he forsook the orderly groves of conventional scholarship for the bohemian existence of a freelance writer. He was christened Charles McSweeney but adopted the name Diarmuid Ua Duibhne when he began to write. Ua Duibhne was not lacking in talent and might have succeeded as a writer or critic had not some evil star fated him to take lodgings in the same building as John Ignatius O'Flynn. O'Flynn hounded and haunted him with manuscripts and invitations to his opening (and usually closing) performances. At first our critic was amused (he began to append the letter P. to his name in mockery of O'Flynn's L). Later he became depressed to the point of being disillusioned about the literary life. He returned to the university, completed his doctorate, and currently teaches in an elementary school in rural Ireland. Ua Duibne is an able and worthy fellow and deserves better than to be included in this book.

---

[70] Warrior hero in the Finn Chronicles of Ireland, also renowned as a great lover.

Oedipus with the Oracle on Mount Olympus

DAIRMUID UA DUIBHNE'S REVIEW OF "OEDIPUS LEX"

A play by John Ignatius O'Flynn,

I saw this play last Tuesday in a sense, for it was pushed through my letter box,[71] all four volumes of it, with a note begging me to read and review it. To the best of my knowledge it has never been produced, and to be brutally honest, I believe it never will be. The author is a well-known character about town who describes himself as a playwright. He was thrown out of law school some years ago on failing all his first year examinations for the second time. He has since affected the first letter of the LL.B. degree which he awarded himself, apparently for

---

[71] A letter box is a metal flap in a door. It is used to deliver mail, small parcels, and, occasionally, explosives.

good attendance. He has written a number of plays, all of them on legal themes and none of which have been produced. The author tells me, in his accompanying note, that he hopes to establish himself with this play as a major dramatist and is sanguine about its prospects of being adapted as a musical on Broadway.

This opus is in four acts, each of which would last for a week. I cannot pretend to have read, much less understood, all of it, but the gist is as follows:

In Act One Oedipus, abandoned by his parents at birth and brought up by simple shepherds, sets out to become a lawyer, hoping to return and save his foster parents from a neighboring landowner who was inflicting obscure legal maneuvers on them. He meets two blind brothers, both prophets, called the Seers Roebuck who tell him that he is fated to be the bane of mankind, to murder his father and marry his mother. They also warn him to look out for wooden nickels. For this the seers charge Oedipus fifty drachmae, which turned out at any rate of exchange to be plenty. Oedipus travels on to Mount Olympus where he hopes to study the law. Twenty scenes (and fifty soliloquies) later he arrives there in time for Act Two, some of which I will reproduce so that the reader may have some idea of the substance of this play.

ACT II

SCENE. - Mount Olympus. The Delphian Oracle[72] is peeping from behind a rock.

Chorus. [Law students accompanied by Aeolian Harp[73]]

Longing for lore we cross the wine-dark sea[74]
From Cos and Io and sunny Thessaly.

---

[72] O'Flynn has confused Olympus with Delphi but it amazing he managed to locate it in Greece.
[73] The only harp of which O'Flynn was aware is the Dublin beer of that name.
[74] A real descriptive term from Greek poetry!!!!!

Our homes we left to sail in boat and coracle[75]
To learn law at Olympus from the Oracle.

Oracle. Before the law fall ye upon your knees
And chant the holy lesson if you please
Today recite the principles that tether
The fibers of the Universe together

Chorus. [They chant]

These dooms the hand that stretched the heavens' span
Hath written in the heart of every man.
First what is right each man should strive to do.
Then render unto every man his due.
Third is the duty to preserve life.
Fourth earthly needs, your children, home and wife.
Fifth and above all you must seek the truth.

Oracle. Hold your noise - who is this comely youth?

[Enter Oedipus.]

Oracle. Fair youth do you come to learn the law? And have you got
what it takes?

Oedipus. I've got five hundred drachmae.

Oracle. That'll do.

[Takes his money and hands him his diploma.]

Oedipus. You mean that's it?

---

[75] A small sturdy boat framed with tree branches covered with hides. It is reported that St. Brendan
the navigator crossed the Atlantic to America in one.

Oracle. Of course, the knowledge of the law is to know what is just and good. Look deep into your own heart, and you will find there the good, the true, the beautiful and the just. These are the goals; the rest is but the means.

Oedipus. But no books? No exams?

Oracle. It is enough to have learned the heart of the matter here.

Oedipus. I will go then at once and set up practice; where should I begin?

Oracle. Try Thebes

Oedipus. Thank you, I will.

Oracle. Via et Vale.[76]

SCENE. - *The road to Thebes.* **Oedipus** *meets a* **Stranger.**

Stranger. What would you?

Oedipus. I would go to Thebes and be a lawyer.

Stranger. You picked a good time, they are revising their General Statutes. What do you know of the law?

Oedipus. I have looked into my soul and seen there the principles of good and evil.

Stranger. And what are they?

Oedipus. The five basics of Natural Law.

Stranger. What? Who told you that?

---

[76] Latin on Mount Olympos??

Oedipus. The Oracle on Mount Olympus. I admit that I don't understand them very well.

Stranger. Fool! The truth is simple. Good is pleasure and evil is pain.

Oedipus. That does seem simple. Excuse me, I have to go and see somebody.

SCENE. - Back on Mount Olympus.

Oracle. Returned so soon?

Oedipus. I want my money back.

Oracle. Why, was what I taught you not good?

Oedipus. It was useless. All that nonsense about looking into my soul to find the good when I only needed to know that the good was pleasure and evil pain.

Oracle. Was it a little fellow with a scraggly beard who told you this?

Oedipus. Why yes.

Oracle. [*Bitterly*] Jeremy Bentham again. And you believed him?

Oedipus. It seemed self-evident. If I wish to do something it must please me in some way or other, so it necessarily causes me pleasure.

Oracle. But If the good is pleasure I need only do what **I** please, not what I ought.

Oedipus. It would seem so.

Oracle. Then there would be nothing right or wrong.

Oedipus. Apparently.

Oracle. No rights?

Oedipus. So it would seem.

Oracle. And there is no reason for anyone to do anything if they don't wish to.

Oedipus. Excuse me, I will go and try again.

Oracle. Try Corinth this time.

SCENE. - The road outside Corinth.
Oedipus meets another Stranger.

Second Stranger. Whither, youth? And for what purpose?

Oedipus. To Corinth to practice law.

Second Stranger. Timely, they are preparing a new constitution and might value your help. How would you proceed?

Oedipus. I suppose **I** will have to look deep into my own soul again and try to see the unchanging matters of right and wrong.

Second Stranger. But what if other people find something different in their soul?

Oedipus. I had not thought of that. I had supposed all men would have their souls stamped in much the same way

Second Stranger. A supposition, **I** assure you.

Oedipus. You must be one of the skeptics my adopting mother warned me about. There can be no constitution nor indeed law if all do not share the same values.

Second Stranger. I am no skeptic; for everyone shares one value at least.

Oedipus. And what is that?

Second Stranger. Each wants his own way, or as much of it as he can get.

Oedipus. So?

Second Stranger. Well then, if every citizen knows what they want, a compromise can be reached between them which will be fair.

Oedipus. What do you mean by fair?

Second Stranger. If I am given as much of my own way as is possible consistent with the wishes of everyone else, this would be fair, would it not?

Oedipus. I would certainly accept it as such.

Second Stranger. So a lawgiver simply has to adopt an impartial stance and imagine the various citizens each with their own preferences bargaining for the best deal that they can fairly expect. The resulting agreement is the law.

Oedipus. A sort of compact or contract?

Second Stranger. Exactly.

Oedipus. Excuse me, I must talk to someone.

SCENE. - Mount Olympus.

Oracle. Back again?

Oedipus. Yes, I want my money back.

Oracle. What is your complaint this time?

Oedipus. The course was deficient. I was not told the true basis of law.

Oracle. Which is?

Oedipus. Law is based upon a fair bargain struck between competing interests and values, in other words a compact.

Oracle. Someone told you this one too?

Oedipus. Well - yes!

Oracle. A thin balding man with glasses and a shirt bearing the insignia "How 'bout them Harvards?"[77]

Oedipus. The very one.

Oracle. [*Aside*] Janis Rawis at it again. [**To Oedipus**] You consider this better than "the most happiness for the greatest number" that you fell for last time?

Oedipus. Much better. That theory, besides its other defects does not protect minorities.

Oracle. Could the majority also not make a compact disadvantageous to minorities?

Oedipus. Conceivably, but as the Massachussetsian Moralist explained it to me[78], the legislators imagine how they would feel if they were a member of each group in turn, however small, and try to obtain the best possible share for that group even if it should only be a minority of one.

Oracle. But why should the legislators wish to be fair to that small group or minority of one, when such partiality might displease the majority and cost them their office,[79] particularly if the minority were unpopular?

---

[77] O'Flynn has of course no more idea of the appearance of Rawls than man in the moon.

[78] In half a volume of turgid prose from which the reader has been mercifully spared..

[79] According to Rawis, rational self-interest is the only basis required for a theory of justice

Oedipus. I believe they are supposed to imagine that they are not born yet and that in the future might be born a member of that group or be that minority of one.

Oracle. But this is a fiction, of course, since all active legislators are already born.

Oedipus. True.

Oracle. So we still do not know why a legislator should care about the fate of minorities?

Oedipus. I certainly cannot answer this question.

Oracle. Suppose further that we are all hovering in some place and time waiting to be born. Why should we not gamble on being born into the majority and so favor them?

Oedipus. The chances of being born into the majority are certainly greater.

Oracle. So such a chance might be considered rational - a sensible choice by a cool deliberate person.

Oedipus. It appears so to me. Such a one might well prefer good odds that they would have all that they wish rather than imperil the chances of this favorable lot in life merely to guard against the unlikely event of being born into a very small minority.

Oracle. So then rights, particularly of minorities, cannot be guaranteed by theories which treat right and wrong as matters of personal taste, whether pleasure or some other kind.

Oedipus. Apparently not.

Oracle. So gaze deep into your own soul

Oedipus. Wait a minute. How do I know that my values will be the same as everyone else's, as the Bostonian Brain so penetratingly disputed?

Oracle. In your experience of men have you not found in all a respect for virtue, family, truth, life, etc.?

Oedipus. Save in the case of the landowner who oppressed my foster parents, that is so, and he was admittedly an unusually perverse individual.

Oracle. And do not the arrangements of the world suggest the work of an orderly mind appreciative of beauty and order and virtue?

Oedipus. Indeed, the shepherd who initiated me into the mysteries used frequently to say this in his weekly diatribes, and it always seemed to me to be most plausible.

Oracle. Well then, is it not most reasonable to assume that the general beneficent ideals of mankind are the true values, and to shape the law to these ends?

Oedipus. Especially since there appears to be no viable alternative.

Oracle. Well, go then and practice - try Athens this time. May I suggest that you enter the city by night and if any conversationally disposed person stops you on your way into the city, brain them instantly with your staff.

. . . .

Act **III** describes the further adventures of Oedipus, consisting of forty-three scenes filling a volume and half, all of them much like the above. I felt compelled to read to the end as I was curious about the prophesies of the Roebuck brothers concerning Oedipus killing his father and marrying his mother. Somewhere about scene twenty-three Oedipus marries a female law student (who can hardly have been his mother), and the only person he killed was a poor fellow who was hanged subsequent to a brilliant but unsuccessful defense by Oedipus. This all goes to show that you can't depend on anything you get from the Roebuck Seers for fifty drachmae.

In short, I cannot recommend this play. Someone (probably O'Flynn himself) writing a review of one of his previous plays in this magazine, described it as a "crie de coeur," a cry for help. I think that the author is indeed in need of help and trust that he will be persuaded, or even required, to accept it in the near future.

Dairmuid ua Duibhne, M.A., P.[80]

COMMENT

1. This fiction is directed at prudential theories of law, theories which base law not on justice or the divine will, but rather on more accessible things that we can understand without recourse to moral principles or theology. Such notions are called prudential theories, in the sense of mere prudence, the sort of caution that ordinary persons, without moral or religious principles, might use to persuade themselves to behave in a socially acceptable way, for example agreeing that "honesty is the best policy".

2. The two prudential theories selected here are Bentham's utilitarianism, based on pleasure/pain principles where good law achieves the greatest happiness for the greatest number of people; and John Rawl's THEORY OF JUSTICE, based on the notion of a fair compromise where each individual gets as much of what they want as they could reasonably expect, given that other people also have wishes.

3. These two theories, based on ordinary experience, were expected to be more practical and more objective, more likely to lead to reliable conclusions without too much argument.

4. Unfortunately, as the fiction brings out, these prudential theories do not deliver what they promise, and give rise to more objections than the moral and theological theories that they were designed to replace.

---

[80] I gave up on the Ph.D program after one year. D ua D

5. Bentham's utilitarianism is riddled with problems. To begin with, he defines pleasure as a sensation, which ignores the fact that enjoyment is only occasionally accompanied with sensations: we are usually too absorbed in what we are doing to feel anything. It is also difficult, indeed near to impossible, to measure pleasure, especially in large populations. Counting noses is a simple way round this problem but not an answer, since it is notorious that what people vote for is often not what they will like in the long run with more experience. But the greatest problem in utilitarianism is the protection of minority interests, since the interest of the majority can and often does, run counter to those of minorities.

6. Modern utilitarians have various ingenious remedies for these ailments, but the problems seem to remain[81]. Bentham himself more or less abandoned the theory for practical purposes and substituted a list of some thirty five good things by means of which his reforming codes of law should be measured.[82]

7. John Rawls, originally, like most economists, a utilitarian, later broke away from it entirely, mainly because of its failure to protect minority interests. But his theory too turned out to have serious problems.

8. To begin with the scheme is no easier to work than Bentham's. When I present my initial proposal to individual A, it may not be all that A wants and a modification is suggested which individual B may not find entirely to their taste and wish to amend, and so on. And this is not just a theoretical problem, for looking after the interests of everybody is not likely to produce a workable arrangement. It is like a bill fighting its way through the legislature which ultimately becomes nothing like the original and stripped of all the advantages that it was hoped to produce.

9. But the principal objection to Rawls' theory is that it cannot take us where Rawls wishes to go. He wishes to base law on good liberal

---

[81] Nicholas Rescher, DISTRIBUTIVE JUSTICE 1966

[82] In this goal directed morality he does not claim that his values are derived them from any moral theory, though he believes that they ultimately rest on his pleasure/.pain principle. This sounds almost like the pragmatic view of the legal maxims,, namely that are not Natural Law principles but just empirical statements about the actual goals and ends of each department of the law. They cannot be deduced from Natural Law principles though they can be supported and justified by them.

principles which almost every normal person would agree with. But in the best known version of his views, the little angels base their agreements not on notions of right or wrong or concern for their fellows, but purely on rational self-interest, the actual wants of each individual. The arguments that he uses are, not surprisingly, somewhat suspicious, with subtle makeovers in the meaning of ordinary words. Fairness is defined, for instance, as when each individual gets their own way or as much of it as they can hope to get. But we ordinarily mean much more than this by fairness. It involves consideration for other persons. Similarly concern for the handicapped and people at the bottom of the heap who cannot compete, is based on the concern of the little angels that they might be born into that situation. However, that fear can hardly be enough to make us sacrifice serious financial interests, for it is extremely unlikely, though not totally impossible, that any one of us will end up at the bottom of the heap. But a more important question is whether rational self-concern is really the reason why we wish to help the unfortunate: hardly. In short what this objection amounts to that if you start with rational self-interest, you can't hope to reason your way to liberal values which, as commonly understood, are other-regarding. In short "you can't get there from here"[83]

10. The most obvious cure for the problems of Rawls' theory of justice would be to get a higher starting point, to raise the veil of ignorance and allow the little angels have some unselfish values. But this would be to sell the pass and allow something like Natural Law values back into the system. This would greatly shorten and simplify the book but it would no longer be prudential and clearly would be contrary to the author's stated intentions.

---

[83] Brian Barry, THE LIBERAL THEORY OF JUSTICE, Oxford 1972.

PART SIX

NATURAL LAW

Considering the view that value statements, including those of a moral nature, cannot be reduced to nor represented as statements of fact or or in terms of general agreement.

OUR AUTHOR

Rev. Samuel McWaddy D.D

Ordained minister, scholar, and university trustee, esteemed as a truly good and great man whose major shortcoming may have been that he turned the virtue of meekness into a vice. Neither ridicule, scorn nor abuse could make this worm turn. There is also a faint suspicion that his famous meekness was a sham, a device that he cultivated to infuriate his enemies. Prominent among these was Judge Burghermeister chairman of the board of trustees in Algonquin college. "Name that Norm" is attributed to Dr. McWaddy with some confidence and may have been a proposal for a Law Day Program to follow up on Judge Burghermeister's disastrous "Ballet of the Books" which had bombed out so gloriously the previous year. If so, it was probably intended as one more sly thorn in the flesh (and nail in the coffin) of the worthy judge.

A game show in Heaven

NAME THAT NORM

A Heavenly Game Show For Translated Lawyers
By
Reverend Samuel McWaddy, D.D.

This manuscript was found among the papers of the late Dean John Austin Goodman of the Algonquin J. Calhoun School of Law. Its authorship is disputed but most of the trustees, and who should know better, believe that is comes from the vitriolic pen of the Reverend Samuel McWaddy, longtime trustee of the University. It was written, they say, as a follow-up to Judge John M. Burghermeister's disastrous "Ballet of the Books" and intended to be presented the following year as part of the Law Day celebrations. Critics of this view, the minority, object that the Reverend McWaddy would surely not have penned an anonymous work and also point out a degree of irreverence which would be quite out of character, they say, for such a devout and good man as the Reverend McWaddy. The majority however maintain that Reverend Samuel was a sly dog who assumed the mask of infinite meekness to aggravate and harass his associates, particularly Judge Burghermeister. The latter, though a good man, was of a choleric and irritable disposition and thus a perfect target for such attacks. The play, they say, was mailed anonymously to the law school in the hopes that it would come to the attention of the trustees and be performed. The plan was machiavellian in the extreme. If it was taken as a joke it would be at the judge's expense; if presented on stage and failed it would have the same significance. If, however, it was presented and succeeded; it would embarrass and infuriate Mr. Burghermeister most of all. This diabolical scheme however failed. The manuscript was placed on Dean Goodman's desk for his attention, disappeared without trace among his papers and only surfaced years later when all the affected parties had gone to their reward. The ways of providence may be strange and wondrous, but they sometimes work.

INTRODUCTION.

Narrator: Much speculation has been devoted to the question of what angels do to pass the time (or rather eternity) in Heaven. Every age and culture has its own ideas. The harp, a popular instrument in days gone by, used to feature prominently in descriptions of heaven. But practically nobody plays the harp nowadays and it ought to be quietly dropped from the list of celestial accoutrements. Game shows are the thing now: at least half the population is addicted to them. So the following is suggested as a heavenly entertainment for angels who have been lawyers on earth - assuming any of them make it.

SCENE. The courts above. A rather small audience of angels (wigged and gowned) is seated before a stage. Center stage is a large golden box with jeweled hinges inscribed (in letters of pearl) with the words NATURAL LAW. Enter a great heavenly beast (see Ezekiel, Daniel and the Book of Revelation) called "The Great se*al*.".

The Great Seal: Blessed Barristers, once more we present your favorite game show, NAME THAT NORM!; and here is your heavenly host, Norm Maxim!

[Enter Norm, full-wigged, dressed in scarlet robes covered with sequins, and carrying a menorah.[84] He is cultivating a slight resemblance to Liberace]

Norm Maxim: Good evening gentlemen, or I should say "ladies and gentlemen," for we have no sex discrimination up here or for that matter no ---

[He is drowned out in stamping of feet, boos, and cat-calls.]

We are here to play your favorite T.V. game - NAME THAT NORM, the game where principles pay off and maxims make money. Let's begin by introducing our current champion, Mr. O. Hapgood Day, who has been a winner three weeks in a row. Mr. Day has won many prizes, including the beautiful pair of spectacles he is wearing tonight, made by the Archangel Michael himself out of two old diamond door knobs from the pearly gates. **[Oohs and aahs.]** Now, let us hear it for our current champion Mr. Oliver Hapgood Day. May I call you Happy?

Happy Day: You certainly may, Norm; since after all I am already dead.[85]

Norm Maxim: Quite! - Happy, would you mind telling us, for the benefit of our new viewers, how did you managed to get to Heaven?

Happy Day: I graduated from Campbell.

Norm Maxim: Of course. *Res ipsa loquitur,* right?

Happy Day: **[who speaks French fluently]** Naturellement!

---

[84] A seven branched candlestick.
[85] "Call no man happy until he is dead" (Aesculus)

Norm Maxim: Tell me, Happy, what was your favorite course there?

Happy Day: Jurisprudence.

Norm Maxim: Jurisprudence? Is that a popular subject at Campbell?

Happy Day: They love it.

Norm Maxim: [**To audience.**] Who says liars can't get into heaven! [*Laughter.*] Let's have a big hand for O. Hapgood Day.

[He gets a fair-sized hand at that.]

Norm Maxim: Now let's introduce our first contender, Mr. John Stone from Detroit. Is it true, John, that you were known as "Honest John Stone" by your colleagues in the law?

John Stone: That is a fact.

Norm Maxim: Then I needn't ask you how you got here - it was by honesty, right?

John Stone: Indeed it was. I starved to death.

Norm Maxim: [*Sighing.*] Well, as we say, "*In jure non remota sed proxima causa spectatur,*" right? ("you can't win them all?").

All: [*With feeling*] Right!

Norm Maxim: Let's get on with the game. Now, Happy and John, we've got a wonderful audience here to cheer you on tonight, a small but select group, not like that rowdy horde of lawyers they've got down below. Like I always say, "*Dominium extendat ad coelum et usque ad inferos,*" which as you all know means "If you want a quiet game of dominoes, come to heaven; if you insist on wild parties, you can go to ----"

[More booing and cat-calls.]

Right now they are probably playing "Recite That Rule" down there - I ask you! But blessedly we are maxim lawyers, men of principle, and so we play

[Fanfare from The Great seal] – "NAME **THAT** NORM"

[Faint cheers.]

I will now explain the rules - I mean the principles - of the game. In this box the great eternal and unchanging principles of Natural Law are inscribed on illuminated pages of vellum. I am going to draw them out in their proper order. The contestants will have to name each principle in advance, and then, when I bring it out, tell the audience what it means. Every time you make a right guess or give the correct explanation you get one candle out of my candlestick according to the principle "in vino veritas."[86] If you guess wrong or give an inappropriate explanation the rams horn will be sounded by my good friend here, The Great Seal.

[The Great Seal gives a horrendous demonstratory blast on the biggest ram's horn you have ever seen]

When all seven candles are given out the game is over. Whoever has the most candles is the winner and becomes our champion; the other is of course the loser. Do you understand, John?

John Stone: Of course. *"Inclusio unius exclusio alterius."*[87]

Norm Maxim: [*To audience.*] This kid learns fast. [*Continuing.*] We have some wonderful prizes tonight. First---[*Fanfare from The Great Seal on ram's horn.*] --- No evening choir practice for a whole week. [*Real cheers.*] Second, [*Another fanfare from Great Seal*] sixteen free harp lessons from the Archangel Gabriel himself. We're glad to see him

---

[86] Roughly, "The truth is in the bottle (or box)".

[87] A well-known principle of documentary interpretation. Originally a remark by the Roman jurist Ulpian to his horse when it caught one of its feet in the stirrup. In that context, as here, this maxim means "If you're getting on, I'm getting off"."

in the audience - big hand for Gabe everybody. [*Tepid applause.*] And finally --[*The Great seal surpasses his previous efforts.*] if any contestant gets all seven candlesticks, he gets to skate on the Sea of Glass - any questions? [*None.*] Then we'll start with John. John, I am putting my hand in the heavenly box and bringing out a piece of beautifully illuminated vellum with the first principle of Natural Law inscribed upon it and it is - ?

John Stone: [*Scratching his head.*] Ah--- Um---It's on the tip of my tongue - the Golden Rule.'

[*The Great seal lets fly with the ram's horn right in the challenger's ear.*]

Norm Maxim: Good, John, but not good enough. The Golden Rule relates to social relationships which are certainly the subject of one of the great principles of Natural Law but hardly the first. Would you like to try again?

John Stone: Eh?

Norm Maxim: Our challenger is a bit under the weather it seems, so let's put the same question to our reigning champion – O. Hapgood Day?

Happy Day: Um ---Ah---It's coming, it's - The Ten Commandments.

[**He too loses an ear to The Great Seal,
Sympathetic groan from audience.**]

Norm Maxim: Too bad Happy, but not right. The Ten Commandments are derived from the second order principles of Natural Law which are not immutable but subject to change. Did I get you right, St. Thomas?

St. Thomas: [**Sulkily.**] More or less.

Norm Maxim: Now both champion and challenger have failed and are "*in pan delicto*," which of course leaves the defending champion as the winner. "*In jure potior est positio defendentis*,"[88] right?

All: Right.

Norm Maxim: So O. Happy Day will remain champion. Okay, Happy?

Wilson Day: Eh?

Norm Maxim: Our champion doesn't seem very well either but as we say here "*Fiat justicia ruat coelum*."[89] Now, our next contestant - John Wayne!

[The Duke steps up, splendid with Sheriff's star and six-guns.]

Norm Maxim: You are a lawyer?

John Wayne: No, but I'm a law man.

Norm Maxim: Do you know the first principle of Natural Law?

John Wayne: Yup.

Norm Maxim: And it is

John Wayne: A man's gotta do what a man's gotta do.

Norm Maxim: That's a bit unorthodox. We'll have to check. St. Thomas?

St. Thomas: Well, the correct answer is "Every man following the rule of practical reason ought to do what is right" but ---

Norm Maxim: I suppose that's close enough.

---

[88] If the first horse is disqualified the one coming in next is declared the winner.

[89] Meaning that if the sky falls on you, you probably deserved it.

[Hands John Wayne one candle.]

Norm Maxim: Now, can you tell me what it means?

[big John starts to draw his gun.]

Norm Maxim: Not that way, just tell me in words what it means?

John Wayne: Well, let me see. It means that you have to respect all those things that your daddy taught you.

Norm Maxim: Such as?

John Wayne: Such as motherhood, honesty and telling the truth and only hurting the really bad guys like stagecoach robbers and Viet Cong.

Norm Maxim: St. Thomas?

St. Thomas: Ah well ---

Norm Maxim: Close enough. Now the second principle.

John Wayne: Well I always say that everybody, especially bad guys, should get what's coming to them.

Norm Maxim: St. Thomas?

St. Thomas: The usual expression, as Plato and the Stoics expressed it, is "Render to every man his due," but **I** suppose---.

Norm Maxim: Thank you, St. Thomas. Now, Mr. Wayne, you are doing well so far; do you want to take a chance and go for the big secret prize?

All. [vi et armis[90]] Go for it!

---

[90] "With force and arms i.e. enthusiastically.

John Wayne: I'll go for it.

Norm Maxim: Great! Then can you tell us the next three subsidiary principles of Natural Law in proper order?

John Wayne: Well, you've gotta have respect for life ---.

Norm Maxim: Good ---.

John Wayne: And fulfill your ordinary duties well - look after your family and all that..

Norm Maxim: Great! And ---.

John Wayne: And my daddy always told me to respect the truth.

[The Great Seal really overdoes it here with a fanfare on the ram's horn. He flops off in pain, supporting his hernia with one flipper.]

Norm Maxim: Wonderful. Well, it looks like we've got a winner here. Let's open the box and make sure.

[*He reads.*]

Do what is right
Render to every man his due.
Preserve life.
Fulfill normal duties to family etc..
Seek the truth.

Yes, I think you had them all in there somewhere. So, Mr. Wayne, you get a week off choir practice - the other choir members will be pleased - and here are your skates. As a special prize, you get to ride on the four horses of the Apocalypse; I'm sure the four horsemen won't mind either. So let's have a big hand for this week's big winner, Mr. John Wayne.

All. [In chorus.] Affirmed.

Norm Maxim: And you'll all be back here next week at the same time for another session of NAME THAT NORM - right?

ALL: Wrong!!!

AMEN!

COMMENT

1. This fiction concerns the doctrine of Natural Law, i.e., that some things are good and others bad in themselves, no other reasons are needed.
2. The "heavenly box" is a standard criticism of Natural Law, namely how do you know that there is a box in heaven and even if it exists how do you know what is in it? This criticism, commonly supposed to be dispositive, is actually misplaced, Natural Law does not exist in heaven but is rather indelibly imprinted in human nature. John Wayne's image as a bluff and tough ordinary person is a good example. He may not be a moral philosopher but he knows right from wrong.
3. The contrast of the heavenly lawyers with the more numerous crowd down below, is also in point. Multiplying regulations without carefully connecting them to the ends that they should serve is bad lawyering and a major problem in administrative law. The critical legal studies people may have one thing right anyway when they say that "hell is full of regulations."
4. The axiomatic nature of moral principles is similar to David Hume's point about our belief in the existence of such things as external colored objects; other persons; and objective cause and effect. We do not perceive such things directly. Light reflects from objects and enters our eyes where it is encoded in the retina and transmitted in code to the brain. We cannot argue from the information in the brain to the existence of trees and people and so on in the real world. But we not only believe that they are out there, the belief is unshakable:

try as we may we cannot but believe that they are objectively present..
As Hume commented "Nature is stronger than Reason." In the same
way we cannot avoid the main principles of Natural Law. We just
cannot bring ourselves to accept that it is OK to murder, lie, neglect
our families or our duties to our fellow human beings. We may not in
practice follow these moral mandates but we cannot shake ourselves
free from them. Even Charles Manson knew that his murderous
doings were morally wrong.

5.   Note that the contents of the box are general principles not particular
rules. This is another misunderstanding of Natural Law which has led
many to doubt its existence. For since ideas of right and wrong differ
markedly from one culture to another, how can Natural Law exist: it
is supposed to be the same everywhere, in all ircumstances and with
all human beings[91]. But though the rules vary, the principles remain
the same. So in the old Eskimo society, in time of dire need, it was
allegedly customary to eat the children, starting with the youngest
who had less invested in them and less to contribute to the needs of
the family. Even if this was so, and many Eskimos questioned it, the
principle is the same: the parents are saving the lives of the whole
community. The other standard example supposed to disprove the
existence of Natural Law, is the old Polynesian custom where the
main capital offence was failing to apologize to a seal after the hunter
had killed it. But here again the principle holds good. The islanders
believed that failing to apologize to the seal would cause all the other
seals to move away and so the community would starve. Rules may
vary but the underlying principles remain the same.

6.   St. Thomas indeed noted that though the principles remained intact,
the rules deriving from them were very variable due to changing
circumstances or even changes in moral opinion. Mining, fishing,
felling timber and all sorts of other commercial practices that were
once considered normal are now held to carry serious environmental
evils.

7.   Another cause of moral uncertainty is conflict between two
valid principles. Old philosophical conundrums along these lines

---

[91] *Ubique. ibique et ab omni* as the Roman jurist Ulpian put it.

hypothesized a homicidal madmen coming to your door and asking where Mr X is (he is hiding behind the door), Do you tell the madman the truth or lie in order to save X's life.? Such examples must be so rare as to be nonexistent. But conflict between moral principles is far from rare. Important business executives, military commanders, lawyers and government officials and even ordinary persons, frequently feel obliged to suppress and even deny the truth. If their reasons for doing so are self serving, this is reprehensible; but what if they are doing it for the public good? Real moral dilemmas can occur every day for most of us. Even when the decision we feel obliged to make is clearly right, crossing the moral line can still leave us with guilt. The pilot and crew who dropped the atomic bomb on Hiroshima felt that it was not only right but necessary in order to save countless lives, and furthermore that it was their duty as military officers who have been given an order. Yet what did they feel afterwards? Doing what is right in such circumstances comes at a price.

8. The ethical theories we have so far considered all have their problems and this goes for Natural Law as well as the prudential varieties. But when they are considered side by side, clearly some form or other of Natural Law is to be preferred.

PART SEVEN

GRAND FINALE

Legal literatureand legal science

Grand finale - the Ballet of the Books

THE BALLET OF THE BOOKS

By
Justice John Marshal Burghermeister

The following are excerpts from the minutes of the February 16ᵗʰ special meeting of the Trustees of the Algonquin J. Calhoun School of Law. Dr. Van Veeghens, President of the University, in the chair.

The meeting was called to discuss Mr. Justice Burghermeister's proposal for the celebration of Law Day. Mr. Burghermeister stated that he felt that previous efforts in this regard had not attracted the attention which he felt the day deserved. The usual public lectures, quite frankly, were a "flop" and something with more "life" in it should be attempted to draw attention to what, so far as the law school was concerned, was "the day of days" in the year. He further stated that he happened to have with him, on his person, a proposal to enliven the same. *(producing a bulky manuscript from a side pocket)* It was, he said, a ballet and besides being more likely to draw a crowd, the affinities between the dance and the law were well known. He had always felt in his career as a judge the need for balance and the ability to walk a fine line, and had drawn much professional inspiration from the ballet.

The Reverend Dr. Samuel McWaddy, Vice-Chairman of the Board of Trustees, warmly seconding the proposal, remarked that in the past, dancing at the end of a rope had also frequently been associated with the law. He added, in response to a question by the chairman, that he was not trying to be funny and asked pardon if his remark has offended anyone. The proposal was adopted unanimously, although a number of the trustees had to excuse themselves and leave before the vote, due to pressing prior engagements.

Excerpt From the Campus Newsletter
"The Smoke Signal"

An audience of several persons was treated on Friday last (Law Day) to a new ballet which we understand was written and choreographed by Mr. Justice Burghermeister, Chairman of the Law School Board of Trustees.

The music, a series of well known tunes, was provided by the school marching band under the leadership of its conductor and principal baton twirler, Daphne (Toots) McDaniel. The dances were performed by members of the Student Bar Association and the "Law Spouses." Refreshments were provided by the Association of Female Parents of the Law Spouses (AKA Mothers-in-law).

In the first act the chorus, or whatever passes for the chorus in a ballet, leaped around the stage - jetes and coupes santes I believe are the technical expressions - to represent the primeval disorder, which they did very well. Then **Nous** or "mind" represented by a young lady who had obviously danced before, subdued these elements. After that she struck an arabesque, and two further figures, representing **Religion** and **Philosophy,** appeared behind her and pirouetted round the stage with an occasional arabesque or two of their own. With each "attitude" new figures sprang forth to cavort around the stage to the general admiration of the disorderly elements (played by law students of course). Next came **The Justinian Corpus,** followed by The six books of **Canon Law,** and, finally, at the end of *Act One,* a group of earthy looking individuals, obviously tillers of the soil, shuffled into a huddle and gave being to a grey bearded figure in white robes, who, I understand, represented **Customary Law.**

Following tea and sandwiches provided by the Mothers-in-law, Act Two got under way. This opened with a dance depicting the struggle between bad King John and the Barons followed by the appearance of **Magna Charta,** who pirouetted and arabesqued around the stage with two other characters called **Tyranny** and **Injustice.** The Act concluded with Chief Justice Sir Edward Coke contending (dance-wise) with King James I. One arabesque later the **Bill of Rights** appeared, and the act ended.

I have not mentioned of course the large number of books that kept emerging at odd times. There was **Bracton's Customs,** as I recall, **Littleton's Tenures,** and various **Year Books.** there were a lot of them circulating around by the end of the second act.

The third and final act began with the Pilgrim fathers and mothers doing glissades (I believe that's the expression) from right (England) to left (America) to the sounds of The New World Symphony. Sir William Penn, who strongly resembled James I in Act II led the troupe, with **Magna Charta** and Lord Coke jeteing and pirouetting all over the place. Almost on arrival a new book - the **United States Constitution -** leaped forth and gave a vigorous performance to the tune of America the Beautiful.

At this point things livened up somewhat. One dance followed another in quick succession: cowboys and indians, saloons and sheriffs, buffalo hunts, and ethnic immigrants (jig to "When Irish Eyes are smiling"??). There was even a tremendous pas de deux by J. Edgar Hoover and John Dillinger, ending with the death of the latter to the sound of a roll of drums (machine gun fire). Next came the industrial revolution, a strike, and the civil war (or whatever they call it down here). This featured Abe Lincoln's Gettysburg Gavotte which was remarkable, to say the least.

And all the time there were books - all sorts of books - carried around by the lawyers. One frontier lawyer (young Abe Lincoln, I guess) carried **Blackstone's Commentaries** on one shoulder and **Greenleaf's Evidence** on the other. Finally the lawyers joined together in the A.B.A., picked up all the books, whirled around in a kind of a Czardas (to Liszt's Hungarian Dance) and ended up in a tableau with the Bible and Plato somewhere around the foundation and Justice (complete with blindfold, scales and sword) at the pinnacle. Unfortunately, the pyramid became unstable and collapsed. Justice and the Bible had to be taken to the hospital. We heard later that Justice had a fractured clavicle, but the Bible got away with a sprained ankle.

This was certainly a remarkable event. As Dr. Van Veeghens remarked, it told the story of our law in a way that no one could possibly forget. The performance made a great impression on me. Your reporter had not realized there were so many law books and has decided to switch from pre-law to pre-med.

Dr. Van Veeghens concluded his remarks by thanking Mr. Justice Burghermeister for his efforts and inviting the remaining audience to come backstage for further refreshments. Sorely needing refreshing, I did.

Finis

COMMENT

1. This fiction represents the organization of the law during its history and quite correctly focuses on the importance of books. The story of the law has largely been the tale of the various books that were written to put the law in some sort of order for the convenience of its practitioners. Very early came the Year Books, initially the notebooks made by apprentices, jotting down anything happening in the Royal courts that they thought was interesting. These eventually became professional court records. The earliest books were rather curious works, almost political pamphlets. reacting

(largely with disapproval) to the changes in the previous Anglo Saxon law made by the development of the Norman Royal courts at Westminster. The first real law book was Littleton's TENURES, describing the originating writs of the developing common law. Bracton's COMMENTARIES carried on the same trend and went through several editions to keep it up to date. And the story goes on. One very notable work was Blackstone's COMMENTARIES ON THE LAWS OF ENGLAND, published in the latter part of the eighteenth century. This was basically Judge Bracton's lectures given to teenage students in Oxford to enable them to go home and function as local magistrates in their parent's estates. Bracton was a magnificent teacher (he had to be) and his works were so lucid that they became the standard legal text carried around by the early American lawyers, who had no previously established law to guide them. These books were not merely descriptions of the law. They were organizing law for legal purposes, in other words they were doing legal science. Some of the earlier books could hardly be described as scientific works, for instance where the actions at law were merely listed alphabetically. But generally they followed some pattern that was considered scientific at the time. From classical Roman through medieval times the pattern was Platonic, with cases and details being organized under general principles (like Plato's forms) .In the latter part of the nineteenth and early twentieth centuries the paradigm of science changed, largely following the emergence and prestige of the empirical sciences such as chemistry. The great physicists, such as Galileo and Isaac Newton were, for the moment, relegated to the back burner and described dismissively by the empiricists as "armchair scientists", which indeed they were and none the worse for that. Law, as usual, took its lead from the current predominant science. Austin, following the empiricist principles of the chemists, introduced the idea of descriptive jurisprudence[92], and the American Legal Realists went even further, reinterpreting the science of law in terms of radical empiricism, sticking close to facts

---

[92] Austin of course intended the description only to exclude improving the law, but he was taken later to remove all value statements. This is an entirely different point which Austin explicitly rejected, talking of principles.

and avoiding theory as much as possible. Herman Oliphant indeed, the principal spokesperson of the movement, was quite explicitly a radical empiricist in his methodology, avoiding theory as far as possible and proposing to reorganize case law into a series of little sets, where small particular groups of facts uniformly led to the same legal conclusion. This proposal was virtually impossible to carry out at that time, though the later development of computers made it just barely feasible. But the development of computer programs also made more complex mathematical arrangements normal and the complex mathematical sciences of astrophysics and submolecular chemistry became the new paradigm for science. Caution was no longer a virtue and imagination and daring hypothesis were deemed desirable as surer roads to scientific progress.

2. Law now has a new task of coming in line with the methodology of the new mathematical sciences, not by imitating them, but rather, taking a broader approach, providing a complex hierarchical organization for legal materials. This is not really new since more than one legal thinker has at least dreamed of something along these lines. Austin, so far from being a radical empiricist, talked of general principles[93] and Roscoe Pound listed the sorts of items that might form the units of a hierarchically arranged legal science. Hebert Hart too made a few suggestions along these lines [94] but none of these authors were able to make any serious advance in the direction of complex organization in legal theory.

3. It is suggested here that modern linguistic logic, based on game theory, could provide a way to reintroduce scientific methodology into jurisprudence.[95] Legal theory can be seen as the organization of technical terms in the form of appropriate word games to further legal purposes.

    (i) The most important of these logical games is the algorithm, the organizing principle of computer logics.

---

[93] Austin's alternative name for jurisprudence was juriscience.

[94] Hart for example in THE CONCEPT OF LAW distinguishes first order rules like the rules of inheritance from second order rules which determine how such rules are to be created and managed.

[95] Simple examples of this kind of ordering can be found in the appendices at the conclusion of the book

(ii)   Each term could be assigned a place in a branching diagram,

(iii) Each term would be referenced to illustrative cases. Case discussion should note whether and how the fact patterns of the case fitted clearly into the legal terms (the circles game would apply here). The text could also be referenced to other materials such as legislation, books and journal articles.

(iv)   If applying the cases to fact situations involving more than one factor, a factors game might be introduced.

(v)   In view of the importance of purposes in interpreting language (a vital consideration in language philosophy) each game should be accompanied by a list of the values that it is deemed to serve. For instance, in the case of battery, the two important values would be protection from physical injury and from insult. This would explain why forcibly removing a book from the hand of a customer in a book store was properly held to be a battery, whereas kicking the tires of the car (though it was deemed a battery) should not have been so decided (no injury or reasonable apprehension of injury and no insult involved). It would also explain why the principle involved in the case of *Riggs v Palmer*, where a youth who murdered his grandfather in order to prevent him making a new will, barred the lad from inheriting. In a later case, allegedly following this decision, a drunken driver whose wife died in the ensuing accident. was prevented from inheriting her estate. This case, was wrongly decided and later reversed. The purpose in the *Riggs* case was preventing criminal interference with making a will, not just disinheriting the grandson because he had done a wrong thing. Consideration of purposes would have made this clear.

4. Law organized hierarchically along these lines would:

(i)   Help lawyers research case law.

(ii)   Assist legislative committees draft reform proposals. They could of course clearly see the status of the law they were revising, and by considering the values served by each piece of legal apparatus would be able to determine whether any proposed change would be beneficial or not.

(iii) Assist in the analysis of judicial opinions, showing which diagram(s) the court was following, which particular terms they considered relevant, how the opinion fitted into already existing law and, especially if the judge was blazing a new trail, how the decision should be justified in terms of the assigned values.

(iv) Level the playing field for case law presentations by first year law students who, instead of being thrown bodily into the murky waters of judicial opinion to find the holding in the case (often a very obscure matter) might be provided with an algorithm, or given instructions for making them, then proceeding to present the case in a logical manner.[96]

---

[96] I am of course aware of the value of the casebook method in developing the students' ability to think their feet while under fire.

APPENDIX #1
MORE DETAILED NOTE ON
LEGAL FORMALISM

MATHEMATICS, LANGUAGE AND THE LAW
An Introduction to Modern Formalism

PART ONE – GENERAL CONSIDERATIONS

§1. The modern predicament – skepticism about formal logics

This section is about logical form, the way that information should be put together in order to function effectively. It is hardly a prominent concept in law schools today. There are even those who write off any kind of logical form or argument as rationalization or, worse, as a fraudulent exercise used in class warfare to achieve social dominance.[97] This is an extreme and ultimately untenable position, but there is some excuse for it. In the middle ages law was arranged on the model of geometry, with all-important first principles (maxims) from which less general rules could be derived until eventually one could reach one that could decide cases. This method has been largely abandoned but, unfortunately, never replaced by anything better. However, total abandonment of logical form is hardly the proper response. Skepticism about logic shares the common problem of all skeptical arguments, that it uses formal argument of one sort or another to make its case – in short that it saws down the branch that it is sitting on. It would seem to be a better option to take a good look at formal theory and see what place, if any, it has in the study and practice of law.

The first and most obvious place to study logical form is where it originally developed, in mathematics and logic. One can then go on to consider other more modern formal systems, especially computer logics and the logic of language.

---

[97] See earlier discussion of American Legal Realism and the Critical Legal Studies movement.

§2. The classical view - mathematics as a way of knowing reality

Mathematics, especially geometry, may have had its beginnings in Egypt[98], but the theories underlying mathematics developed among the classical Greek philosophers. There were all kinds of philosophers in ancient Greece and its colonies, but those whose reputations have survived were mostly *idealists*[99] that is they believed that mind, not matter, was the most important entity in the universe. Socrates in his final discourse with his friends, reported that as a youth he was delighted when he heard Anaxagoras, one of his great predecessors, say that "mind is king of heaven and earth"[100] epitomizing for him the great importance that the Greeks attached to thinking. The Socratic idealists, seeking for truth beyond mere opinion, were impressed by mathematics which seemed to them to be the most perfect form of thinking, since its axioms were certain and the conclusions properly drawn from the axioms were therefore necessarily true. This confidence in deductive mathematical processes persisted into modern times and is known among philosophers as *rationalism*. To these Greek philosophers, mathematics was a "real" affair. By this they meant that when mathematicians worked with numbers or geometrical shapes, they were not just playing with notions, but studying a real aspect of things, i.e., 1 + 1 = 2 is actually true even though it exists in the intellectual world which cannot be reached by the senses but only by the mind. Two centuries earlier, Pythagoras had said that the universe "is" numbers, and the Pythagoreans were members of a semi-religious order who were said to "worship" numbers.[101] In the middle ages those who accepted this view of mathematics, and they were the dominant party, were known as *realists*, while those who rejected it

---

[98] See §4 infra where Pythagoras, advised by Thales to study mathematics, went to Egypt.

[99] From the Greek ιδεα (idea) meaning thought.

[100] Phaedo 97b. B. Jowett, THE DIALOGUES OF PLATO, vol. II. p.482 (1937). Socrates however comments that Anaxagoras went on to talk mainly about material substances. It is possible, however, that Anaxagoras, like most of the presocratics, was not able to view mind or anything else abstractly and therefore discussed nous, i.e. mind, the moving force of his universe, as if it were a substance.

[101] The Pythagoreans were ridiculed by Plato who reports that they spent their time trying to assign numbers to pebbles of various shapes. They communicated their conviction that numbers were real and important to the Platonists who eventually succeeded in developing mathematical science. Sir Isaac Newton considered himself a Platonist.

and thought that numbers were just labels not necessarily implying the existence of anything, were called *nominalists*. This battle continued into the middle of the nineteenth century when a number of mathematicians, notably Gottlöb Frege, developed game theory.

§3. Mathematics as playing games

Nowadays mathematical truth is described as having to do with form rather than substance. This means that $2 + 2 = 4$ is not a statement about the real world; it has nothing to do with real truth but only with formal truth or validity. A conclusion is valid or correct if the symbols and rules in the system i.e. (2), (4), (+) and (=) are used correctly as laid down in the original definitions. Mathematical systems are thus intellectual constructs; we can make them any way we wish, and formal truth has no necessary connection with reality. The fact that the ledger is formally correct does not mean that there is money in the bank. In short they are viewed as games, like chess or Monopoly or baseball: there are pieces (or players) together with the moves and rules which lay down or define how the game is to be played and won. But the whole thing is formal; no real battles are won and no real money is lost. They are just games.[102]

§4. Special terms – calculus, formal systems and logics

The general term commonly used by philosophers and mathematicians to describe such formal systems is *calculus*. This should not be confused with the differential calculus, a form of mathematics devised by Newton and Leibniz[103] in the seventeenth century, featuring differentiation and integration. As used by logicians and philosophers, the term calculus refers to any kind of symbolic game whatsoever. It covers not only the various kinds of mathematics and formal logic, but also the formal arrangements found in ordinary language (word logics) and artificially created languages such as musical notation, the symbols of science and the technical terms of the law; in short any system using symbols and

---

[102] Wittgenstein commented that if war was really like chess, the generals would study it.

[103] Acting independently of one another. Newton apparently believed that Leibniz had plagiarized his work.

moves. Taken broadly in this sense, the study of and use of such systems is called *formalism*. The term logic is also commonly expanded to be synonymous with *calculus*, meaning a formal system of any kind, not just the formal logic of Aristotle or modern symbolic logic. The terms "computer logic" or "military" logistics carry the same kind of meaning.

§5. The protean forms of mathematical games

An infinite variety of mathematical games can be devised. The older arithmetics used sets of ten units, presumably because we have ten fingers, but there is no reason in the world why we shouldn't use any number we please. Binary arithmetic for example uses only two units, 1 and 0, which makes it most suitable as the basis for computer logics, since the ultimate component of a computer is a switch that has to be either "on" or "off", a fact which can be represented appropriately by 1 and 0. Some mathematical systems use the symbol π (pi)[104], known as the natural number, and it has been found useful in biological research. Currently, research mathematicians often work with picture symbols (icons) rather than numbers or letters since they claim that mathematical processes have become too complicated to be represented as simple quantities or equations. A top hat or any other picture can be used to represent six pages of mathematical transformations. It is hardly surprising then that many computer games are spin-offs from pure mathematical research, developed by the computer geniuses when they went home to play with their children.

§6. Pure and applied calculus systems

Calculus systems, though they are in themselves essentially games, can be applied to real affairs. In fact, any topic that has system or regularity of any sort is apt for formal treatment. A game of one sort or another can be found or invented to represent and organize any database or enterprise which is not totally random. Geometry was applied in ancient Egypt to resurvey the Nile delta every year when the floods had wiped out all the old landmarks. Copernicus and Galileo applied

---

[104] The ratio of the radius to the circumference of the circle, calculated by Archimedes to be 3.1418.

a similar system to explain the movements of the heavenly bodies and the trajectory of cannon balls. An obscure physician devised statistics, a different kind of mathematical game, to standardize the preparations of foxglove tea that he used to treat his patients who had dropsy (heart failure resulting from rheumatoid arthritis).

§7. Applied language games – special languages and legal language

Ludwig Wittgenstein[105] initiated a whole new kind of philosophy by insisting that language was essentially sets of calculus systems[106], word symbols used according to rules, so that it is appropriate to speak of the logic of language. These word games are of course applied for everyday purposes. A pure language system can hardly be imagined. Even the imaginary elvish languages invented by Professor J.R.R. Tolkien are designed for communication, which means that they are applied. How languages began and how they grow and develop are considerable mysteries, but they function as formal systems which can be applied for purposes such as communication, issuing commands, telling jokes, poetic expression, etc..

Besides the common languages, there are the special languages of professions or interest groups. Sometimes these are used as a secret code to keep outsiders from knowing what the group are talking about. London cockney rhyming slang is a good example of this from the past, and current teenage jargon functions in much the same way.[107] Alternatively a language system may be developed and adapted by a group to express rather than to conceal; so stamp collectors, drag-racers and members of other clubs have a language of their own, simple ones perhaps, but which must be learned in order to take part in group conversations. And there are the scientific languages, designed to standardize observation and to facilitate communication between researchers. It will be argued

---

[105] An Austrian engineer who became interested in mathematical philosophy and studied with Bertrand Russell at Cambridge. He became more and more involved in philosophical questions, and his work was a powerful originating force in the linguistic movement in Philosophy.

[106] A general term for any kind of symbolic game. It has nothing to do with Newton's differential calculus.

[107] Philosophers have been accused, not without reason, of creating private languages so that it is difficult to attack their arguments.

here that the special language of the law could and should be included in this last category.

§8. The different kinds of symbols used in calculus systems

Complex artificial calculus systems are important tools employed in most learned professions e.g. science, music and of course law. The symbols employed may be words, mathematical notations, pictograms or even short stories (like video-clips)[108], but the type of symbol chosen is not really fixed in stone and they are commonly interchangeable. Chemists for instance are equally comfortable representing substances by words, letter abbreviations or with pictograms representing molecular structures. Musicians normally work with pictograms but can describe individual notes and all sorts of other musical entities with words.[109] Word calculus has always been the preferred logical tool of lawyers but law too can be translated into other symbolic forms. The advent of the computer and computer logics indeed has demonstrated that most things can be ultimately represented by binary mathematical logic using only the symbols 0 and 1 and a few simple transformational rules.

§9. The essential elements of an applied calculus system

There are three things that must be attended to in order to develop or interpret an applied calculus system.[See earlier diagram]

1. The system must be properly set up with the symbols and the rules clearly defined; and it must be internally self-consistent.
2. The things or the enterprise to which the system is being applied must be clearly identified and capable of being organized.
3. The purposes or goals of the application must be indicated and thereafter kept in mind when the calculus is being applied.

---

[108] Much of our thinking is carried out using visual symbols, picture logics of one sort or another. One can even consider short stories or video clips to be useful symbols, seeing which scenario best fits the facts before us. This short story kind of symbol can be used in historical research, seeing which story is most explanatory. It is also much used by courtroom lawyers presenting cases.

[109] I.e., tonic sol-fa.

If these three essentials are not present, the application will not work well, if at all. And each of these elements must be set up properly and used correctly. So if there is inconsistency within the system, ambiguity as to the applications, or if the goals sought are indeterminate, confusion will result.

§10. **Law as applied calculus - normative and descriptive calculus**

We are principally interested here in the formal arrangements of the law and especially legal language. Legal words often resemble and appear identical with terms used in ordinary speech, but there is an important difference. After entering the law these words take on new functions and therefore new meanings. Some of them, indeed, have been through more than one legal system. Many important terms in the common law for instance were imported from Roman Law or Germanic Law or some other legal system, where they already been long in use, and then began another extended life in England and America. And these masses of difficult terms can be represented as formal systems. Leibniz[110], a philosopher and mathematician, perceived this and had no doubt that he could represent Roman Law with a mathematical calculus (though he never in fact did so).

Legal language then can be described as word calculus applied to disputes for legal purposes.[111] Roy L. Stone[112] has argued that legal calculus has a great deal in common with mathematical calculus, and so it has. But there are at least two important differences.

1. The data of the physical scientist to which scientific calculus must be applied, are relatively unchanging, if they change at all: but the social and other conditions to which legal theory must be adapted are altering all the time. Legal science must therefore

---

[110] Gottfried Wilhelm Leibniz (1646-171 developed the differential calculus independently of Newton (who thought that Leibniz had stolen it) and also made some beginnings in symbolic logic. His philosophy (monism) contains his most famous assertion that this is "the best of all possible worlds."

[111] These purposes can properly be summed up and included under the general heading of "justice".

[112] In *The Compleat Wrangler*, 50 Minnesota Law Journal 1966, 1001.

be constantly reviewed since law is, so to speak, shooting at a moving target.

2. More importantly it must be remembered that the purposes of legal calculus and scientific ones are quite different.[113] Scientific calculus states or predicts that certain events will follow others, according to a particular system; and it is a descriptive process. It relates to what is, and we describe its goal as the Truth. Legal calculus on the other hand is designed to advance certain human ends or goals. It represents what ought to be done to further these ends. Its goal therefore is the Good - however that may conceived. We may represent this fact by saying that law is *normative* calculus. This means that law, on its logical-mathematical side, resembles factual scientific reasoning: but since it aims at certain ends or ideal states, law cannot properly be described as true or false, but as good, or beneficial, or the opposite. It is rather like the *practical reason* of the medieval and classical philosophers, seeking "the good", in contrast with pure reasoning which seeks the truth.

§11. Understanding law in terms of calculus

Treating law as applied calculus tells us something about what it means to learn or to know law. Plato and his associates felt that to know anything was to be able to define it verbally, as when Euthephro declared that piety was doing what pleased the gods.[114] On the other hand Savigny and some modern writers have insisted that we show understanding of words not by formally defining them but by using them appropriately.[115]

Both of these apparently opposed views are correct since they are each focusing on a different aspect of language. If we are describing the terms and their inter-relationships in the calculus system itself, verbal definitions are important. For example, a bargain may be defined as the

---

[113] Stone undervalues ends and goals in applying calculus stating that they only enter into the picture when a rule is being formulated. This is rather like Austin's insistence that values are only relevant in legislation not jurisprudence. But Language/logic considerations would hold, rather, that rules cannot be understood or applied apart from their purposes.

[114] Euthephro 6b. Jowett, Op. cit. 388.

[115] See Gilbert Ryle, *Knowing How and Knowing That*, in THE CONCEPT OF MIND, Cambridge University Press (1966).

acceptance of an offer, and a contract as a bargain accompanied by good consideration. Contract theory on its formal side shows us how we may properly move among these terms. But once we go beyond elaboration of the system and begin to apply it to commercial enterprises, explanation takes a different form, usually focusing on the proper use of the terms in practical circumstances.

The third element in calculus theory, ends or purposes, is not always obvious in familiar situations. In describing a smelly factory as a nuisance for instance, we do not normally take the trouble to mention the purposes which the law of nuisance is designed to serve, such as promoting quiet enjoyment of property. These values are always implicitly operative of course, but it only becomes necessary to mention them in unusual or difficult cases. Thus one may say without much discussion of ends or values that an owner has a perfect right to smoke a cigar in his own garden even though it makes his neighbor sick, but no right to raise pigs there. In more difficult or novel situations, however, it is usually necessary to make reference to all the relevant values in order to decide whether something is or is not a nuisance[116]. Or to put this in formal terms; allowing a fact situation to be included under a particular legal term or category ultimately depends on whether doing so would better advance the purposes served by that piece of legal calculus.

Mastery of an area of law is shown then by the ability of the lawyer to define and describe the technical terms and rules, to illustrate their application to cases appropriately, and to decide difficult cases in ways that realize as fully as possible the ends and goals of that part of the law. So to know the law is to know how to use the calculus, to know when and how to use terms like larceny, embezzlement, robbery, breaking and entering, burglary and the like, and to be able to operate confidently and competently in novel and difficult circumstances.

§12. Legal calculus and changing Law

Legal formalism is commonly thought to be associated with ultraconservatism and resistance to legal change, but this is by no means

---

[116] Currently nuisances tend to be defined by government regulations.

necessarily so. Indeed, considering the law as applied calculus, helps us to understand when and how law should be amended to keep up with social change. Legal calculus, as was mentioned earlier, is constantly being adapted to changing circumstances. If the rate of change in society were too rapid, law as calculus would hardly be possible. In a very stable unchanging society, on the other hand, a legal calculus could be perfected and remain fixed for a considerable period of time. Most societies fall in between these extremes, with some areas that are relatively stable and others in a state of flux.[117]

Legal calculus is not usually changed dramatically all at once, as soon as altered circumstances become apparent, but rather slowly and experimentally, a piece at a time. Lawyers do not rush into change, for such improvement as they might gain can easily be compromised by the uncertainty that would result.[118] Well established law is only changed when new circumstances are very pressing and the old law breaks down so badly that the uncertainty inherent in change is outweighed by the inconvenience and harm of an out of date calculus. So the mutation rate in law is slow. A word is added or substituted, the application of a term is extended by analogy, or some value is accorded greater importance (weight). And though the calculus is extended or modified it is still identifiable and the stability of the law is maintained. This process of change or adaptation of a calculus is what Roy Stone calls paraduction,[119] as opposed to deduction or induction; but it is just modifying a calculus to meet new circumstances or get a better result.

§13. The myth of the seamless robe

Mathematical science frequently operates with large and complex sets of symbols and functions, and many of these can in turn be linked together to form huge coherent systems. Yet even Physics, which is an old and very advanced department of physical science, does not by any manner of means present a seamless web, a single calculus in which all

---

[117] Savigny complained that there was no point in trying to codify family law in post-Napoleonic Germany till circumstances were more settled.
[118] A revered maxim states that every innovation in the law creates more disturbance than benefit. See .S.Peloubet, Legal Maxims. N.Y. 1884. 212. Reprinted Rothman. Littleton, Colorado 1985.
[119] See *The Compleat Wrangler*, 50 Minnesota Law Journal 1966, 1001.

the known terms can take their place and work under the same system of rules. A simple example is the coexistence of Huygens' wave theory and Isaac Newton's corpuscular theory of light. The way in which light travels can be explained in terms of either theory but not by both at the same time, they do not mix. Newton's theory is preferred in dealing with cameras and lenses while Huygens' theory is used when we are dealing with radio waves and such like forms of energy. It may be argued that such conflicts, if they can be regarded as such, are the temporary penalties of our ignorance and this may well be so. But since we are ignorant, temporarily or otherwise, we must accept the fact that several calculus systems may apply to the same set of circumstances; that they may not, and often do not mix well together; and that we must learn when and under what circumstances it is better to apply one of them rather than the others. To give a legal example, the same case may sound in either copyright or in eminent domain depending on whether the published materials were appropriated by the state or by a private person: it may even fit equally well into both.[120]

The same lesson may be illustrated in other areas also. The "psychological" and the "physical" languages do not consort well together in the theory of vision. A wave of a certain frequency impinges on neural sensors in the retina and sets up an impulse in the nerve which is coded and transmitted to the brain. All of these items are considered colorless. To ask where color is added is a pointless question in our present state of knowledge. We must content ourselves with changing from a physiological language to a psychological language, or a common sense language, if we wish to speak of color vision.[121]

Biologists have this kind of problem too since teleological language (where bodies and parts of bodies are thought of as having certain functions or purposes) and mechanical language (using biochemical or physical explanations) exist side by side and work together fairly well. Similarly, different and indeed incompatible systems of abnormal

---

[120] So when one publisher used the materials of a rival they were sued in both copyright and eminent domain since they were both using someone else's work and also producing statutory material under a government contract.

[121] A similar problem occurs in mathematical physics where the theory applied in astrophysics does not consort well with that used in submolecular physics.

psychiatry can co-exist reasonably amicably in clinical practice. Clinical psychologists may use a Freudian or a Jungian or an Adlerian system to deal with different patients on the same day, or even the same patient on different days.

The successful use of competing calculus systems depends, of course, on knowing when to use each one and, above all, in being alert to the possibility of inappropriately mixing two competing systems together.

§14. The danger of mixing separate calculus systems together

If the "exact sciences" are unable to produce a seamless web of theory it is unlikely that we shall do so in law. At first glance legal scholars seem to present law as a fairly unified system. They divide it up formally into a relatively small number of compartments, such as the Persons, Things and Relations of Roman Law, or Contracts, Torts etc. in Common Law; and certain unifying themes appear to run through these divisions and tie them together. But a closer examination will reveal that this is not really the case. The formal apparatus of the law is in fact a collection of separate and usually quite small word calculus systems. There are indeed general themes and terms which keep reappearing in topic after topic. These are often terms from common speech, which are of wide application and so tend to get into a number of law games. The notion of fraud, indeed, is so wide in its applications that it is represented in nearly every compartment of the law. But even here it should not be assumed that such terms operate in the same way in each system.

The same word symbols then can reappear in various pieces of legal apparatus, but the meaning and function may be quite different in each of them. The word "possession" for instance occurs both in property and in criminal law but the meaning is subtly different in each case. Sergeant Stevens in his great work on criminal law assumed that the same term had the same meaning in each branch of the law and tried to harmonize the possession required for the crime of theft with that needed to establish title. Not surprisingly he found the task difficult.

Another error is to confuse the meaning of a legal term with that of the same word in a non-legal context. Most legal terms, as has already been noted, were adapted from ordinary language by lawyers, but once absorbed into legal vocabulary they take on new meanings. The term negligence, which in lay language means simply carelessness, is defined in tort law in terms of four formal elements (duty, breach of duty, causation and damage) so that I could be extremely careless indeed and yet not be negligent in the legal sense. Many examples of this kind of error could be given, and for the most part they can be avoided by care and a little common sense. Others are more complex and language/logic principles can be helpful in avoiding confusion. Two examples of this kind of problem will be considered here, the terms *reasonably certain* and *dead*.

§15. "Reasonable certainty" and "beyond reasonable doubt"

The law of evidence admits degrees of proof. For example, "the greater weight of the evidence" is a less stringent requirement than "reasonable certainty" or "certainty beyond a reasonable doubt." The precise meaning of these terms is not easy to establish in absolute terms. Charles Sanders Pierce pointed out, and language philosophers generally agree, that words like "proof" and "certain" are status or achievement words, i.e. they herald a change in status so that someone or something must thereafter be viewed and treated differently. Attaining the age of majority is an obvious example (one can then vote and be sued on ones contracts); other examples are getting married and being declared insane. Such terms signal the end of one kind of behavior or treatment and the beginning of another. The term "proof" operates in just this way. It is a change in the status of a *proposition*[122]when it is deemed sufficiently certain for argument to end and action to begin. Pierce describes this process in terms of probability and his theory of truth is known as *probabilism*.[123] He insists that, outside the formal proofs of mathematics[124] there is no such thing as absolute certainty, only degrees of probability. Probability can be represented as points on a scale or spectrum, running from 0 (completely incredible) to 100 (totally reliable). In between these extremes would lie a series of degrees of probability, ranging from "unlikely", through

---

[122]The terms true or false do not apply to facts but only to factual statements.

[123]Sometimes as "fallibilism"

[124]Mathematical certainty is only conclusive because it is formal i.e. the result is already present by implication in the initial definitions.

"possible", "very likely" and "highly probable". Somewhere along the spectrum it becomes reasonable to act on the proposition. This region may be described as representing "reasonable certainty" and at its upper end we may loosely describe the proposition as true or as a *fact*. I.e. where argument is no longer appropriate.

The term reasonable should indicate to us that the point at which the transition from deliberation to action occurs is not fixed and the same for all disciplines and all purposes, but variable. In the exact sciences the standard of proof will generally be very high, in some cases being very close to absolute certainty,[125] while historians and social scientists may perforce be willing to "accept" theories with a much lower degree of probability.

Understanding the term "reasonable certainty" in this way it is easy to see why legal certainty falls short, and sometimes far short of what would be accounted certainty in other fields. To demand too much would be to immobilize the law; few if any criminals would be convicted and juries in civil trials would almost always have to resort to the Scottish verdict, "not proven." The standard of proof must be scaled down for legal purposes and the trigger point (where legal action becomes reasonable), appropriately located on the probability scale. This is not, of course, like standardizing a precision instrument. It is an approximation reached by striking a balance between the competing values involved. In criminal trials we do not wish to punish the innocent by making conviction too easy. On the other hand, if we raise the standard of proof too high, no criminal will ever be punished. Between these two extremes the standard varies depending on a number of factors, including the magnitude of the offense and the severity of the punishment. Thus in criminal trials, where life or liberty are at stake, the criminal charge must be proved "beyond a reasonable doubt". Even here there may be subtle shifts in the standard; the standard rising a few degrees when someone is on trial for their life, and being relaxed a little for less serious penalties. In the case of

---

[125] Even in hard science there is a sort of hierarchy of probability. At the lower end a notion may be described as a "hypothesis"; as it is deemed more reliable it may called a "theory" and finally may attain the status of a "doctrine". And even here a much lower degree of probability may be enough, in certain circumstances, to make it reasonable to act on a hypothesis or a theory, thus according it a kind of provisional "fact" status.

a traffic offense the standard may be very low indeed. In civil matters the standard is generally less than in criminal trials, and the requisite degree is usually expressed by the phrases "the preponderance of the evidence" or "more likely than not".

It is unpleasant to admit it, but social and economic circumstances can also influence the determination of the level of proof that is required in any case. A stable, wealthy and relatively crime-free society can afford and tolerate a higher general standard of proof than a poor, politically unstable or crime ridden one. Justice, like everything else, must trim its sails to the winds of necessity.

Looking at the term "reasonable certainty" through Pierce's eyes in this way may not make it easy for courts and juries to apply the proper standard of proof, but it does make the standard itself more understandable and less confusing. One is not groping for some absolute touchstone of truth but simply asking whether it is fair and reasonable, given the circumstances, to treat the evidence as sufficient to warrant legal action.

An old ploy, used by some trial lawyers, attempted to confuse courts and juries by treating the action point on a spectrum of probability as if it were something absolute and fixed. If a witness has testified that the accused had been flying at a level of less than 500 feet, Counsel may ask him if he can tell the difference between 400 feet and 500 feet and so on, 100 feet at a time, up to the legal limit of 3,000 feet. The inference, and a patently false one, is that the witness could not tell the difference between 500 and 3,000 feet. Similar examples from cross examinations could be supplied by most trial lawyers. Linguistic logic explains the fallacy in these arguments, and they are easily rebutted by showing other (silly) examples of how such arguments could be employed to make any kind of conclusion by any witness impossible. Indeed on cross examination one could simply ask the witness if they could tell the difference between one hundred feet and three thousand.

PART TWO – APPLIATION OF LANGUAGE LOGICS IN LAW

§16. Legal word logics - the elements game

Suppose that instead of viewing law as a series of sentences, we express it in the form of word-games, with a set of technical terms linked together by formal rules, the equivalent of the pawns, knights and other pieces in chess. It is true that legal rules are commonly expressed as sentences, but this is merely a surface arrangement. The deeper and truly logical structure uses technical terms linked together in word games of various sorts. Roy Stone[126] cites Russell and Whitehead as saying that all mathematics boils down to two key terms "AND", representing conjunction, and "OR" representing dissociation. Both of these games are played out in legal theory. The "AND" game allows the coincidence of a number of subsidiary words, which we describe as elements, to activate a more important term or key-word (like "crowning" a piece which has reached the opponents base line on the checker board). Thus when the familiar tetrad of duty, breach of duty, causation and damage have been shown, the status word "negligence" appears which means that legal action is appropriate.. Each of the elements of course can themselves be status words which become active when certain other elements are produced. Thus causation, one of the elements of negligence, only appears when two other elements, *sine qua non* and *proximate cause* have been shown. When we proceed to consider the element of damages in detail we play a different game, the "OR" game, based on alternation. The term "OR" here is not taken in its exclusive sense of "either A or B, but not both". It is used rather in its weaker logical meaning, where any number of the alternatives may be present but at least one of them must be proved in order to activate the key term, "damage".

Setting this out formally we can say then that in the "AND" game the elements are arranged in the form:

$$A + B + C = X \text{ (the activated term)}$$

---

[126] *The Compleat Wrangler*, 50 Minnesota L. Rev. p.1011 (1966).

whereas in the "or" game they are represented by

$$A \text{ or } B \text{ or } C = X$$

Virtually any area of law can be analyzed in this manner. The basic elements of offer and acceptance together constitute a bargain and this together with consideration constitutes a legally enforceable contract. Procedural law and remedies can be represented in the same way. In organizing law formally by these simple logical devices, we are only doing what the learned and wise in the law have always done; but we are also looking at something strangely modern, the formal logic of language games.

Several other simple logical tools are available and very apt for use in legal theory. These include such devices as intersecting circles, branching diagrams (algorithms) and decisional logics

§17. Useful formal tools – the "circles of Aristotle"

Paired circles have long been used by teachers of logic to illustrate the meaning of the terms "all', "none" and "some". They are sometimes called the "circles of Aristotle" although it is very unlikely that the great philosopher ever used them.

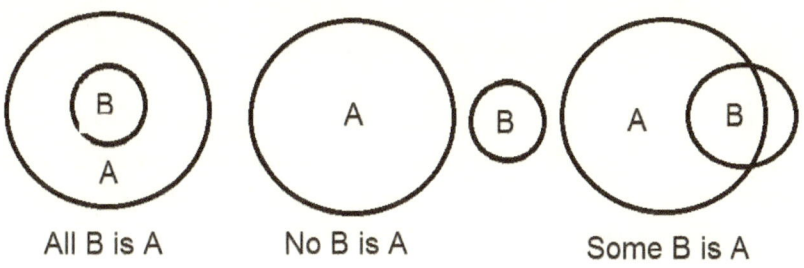

All B is A   No B is A   Some B is A

The circles game as applied to formal logic

This device can be adapted to represent the application of legal terms to fact situations. The large circle represents a legal concept such as "theft" and the smaller circle represents a set of factual circumstances (a case). If a case clearly belongs within the larger circle, the law applies. If it clearly does not belong there the law does not apply. Doubtful cases are represented at the circumference of the circle (as in "Some A is B" above) i.e. it is not clear whether the law applies here or not. Whether a questionable instance will be included or excluded from the circle will ultimately depend on whether considering it "in" or "out" will further or interfere with the objectives of that piece of legal apparatus; this can be clearly seen in the law of nuisance But once a doubtful case has been placed in or out, it may be taken as a precedent so that similar cases should be treated in the same way.

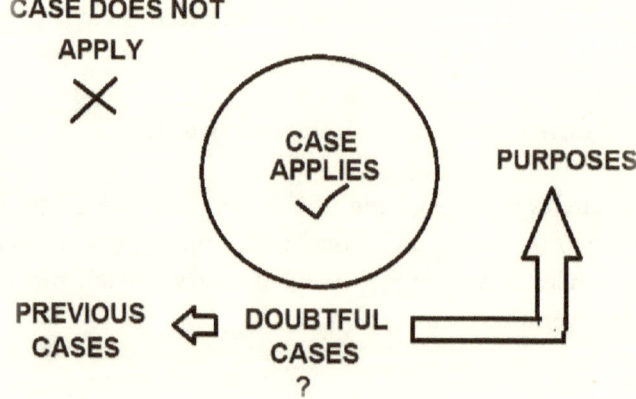

The circles game used to apply legal terms to fact situations.

The circles game is a useful language/logic tool to show how legal terms apply to paradigmatic cases. Thus an illustration may be given where the term clearly applies, followed by a clearly negative example and then perhaps some borderline cases are mentioned. This was a standard technique in medieval law books, for example Bacon's REGULA, and is still used in modern horn books. It is reminiscent of what Wittgenstein calls the "ostensive learning" of language; where the term is mentioned while a finger is being pointed at a thing. For example several blue objects may be pointed out to the pupil as the word is spoken, to teach the meaning of the term "blue".[127]

---

[127]Philosophical Investigations. Op.Cit, Aphorism 6

§18. Other available formal devices –the algorithm

There are a number of simple formal tools that are currently used in other professions, but have somehow failed to attract much attention on the part of legal scholars. Perhaps the most common of these is the branching logic device of the algorithm. This is the basic form of computer logic, based on binary arithmetic with the numbers 0 and 1 representing that a switch is either off or on.[128] The algorithm is used a great deal in medical writing where it can represent all sorts of things such as the steps in a diagnostic process, starting perhaps with a rash and ending with the most likely disorders which may be causing it. It is also commonly used in clinical medicine to select appropriate treatments for particular conditions in individual patients.[129]

The algorithm has much to commend it for use in legal writing.

(i.) First, it is an excellent discipline for legal authors to organize their materials. One is more apt to see confusions and omissions in the diagram than when they are buried in the written text.

(ii.) An existing diagram can act as a check list of items that should be considered when reviewing an area of organized knowledge with a view to applying it for some purpose or other.

(iii.) It is an efficient way to communicate the results of any study to other researchers or professionals. Readers can pick up a total overview of the findings more quickly and more accurately than would be the case with a narrative report. They can also more easily see whether and at what point they may disagree with the writer. They may even indicate the nature of their disagreement by making a change in or a comment on the diagram.

(v) Finally, it is a good way to indicate changes or proposed changes in the law. Two alternative diagrammatic arrangements can be

---

[128] Binary mathematics would appear to allow only two alternatives at each step, but this is not the case. Combinations of 0 and 1 can be used so that any number of possibilities can be represented at each dividing point in the process.

[129] This is not the same thing as using decisional logics which compare alternative values (see §19 infra).

set side by side, showing the difference between the existing and the proposed system

§19. Other available formal devices –decisional logics

Difficult decisions commonly require balancing or weighing of competing values or policies against one another. In medicine, the various factors to be considered in making a decision are often listed, and the items can be formally put together and quantified, The resulting summed number can then be used to suggest that one choice should be preferred to another. Factor lists can be used to choose between competing diagnoses or treatments, for instance to decide whether to treat a condition medically or surgically. Factor lists are also used in business, e.g., to help select the most appropriate person from a short list of applicants for a particular job; or to decide at some point whether to buy or sell shares. Factor lists are regularly used in legal texts, especially Restatements of the Law, at points where polyvalent decisions must be made.[130]These are designed to assist in deciding, for example, whether to require a factory which is polluting the environment to move elsewhere; or to compensate the surrounding home owners for reducing the value of their property; or to pay the costs of moving them away from the nuisance. Similarly, Professor Aaron Twerski has listed ten factors to be considered in deciding whether or not to submit a design defect question to a jury. Unfortunately, in legal texts, the factors are not likely to be helpful since they are simply listed without any instructions as to how they should be used. The medical profession and the business community go further, providing ways of putting the factors together, thus creating a decision-making apparatus. There are two basic ways of doing this.

1. They can be divided into major and minor factors with a formula provided to put them together in a decisional system. These are known as *weighted factor systems* since the major factors weigh more heavily in the decision making process. This method

---

[130]John Austin would hardly agree with this since in his view giving someone discretion to make a choice was like giving them a blank check; there is nothing more to be said once the choice is made.

is used in the Diagnostic and Statistical Manual of Mental Disorders (currently DSM-IV), to help decide which is the most appropriate diagnostic category for a particular set of findings. The diagnostic formula for dementia of the Alzheimer's type (DAT) makes recent memory impairment the one essential major factor. The diagnosis of DAT is then confirmed by the presence of one or more of four minor factors.[131]

2. A different method roughly quantifies the factors by assigning number values to each of them and adding the resulting numbers together to obtain a total score. These are called *scored factor systems*. A simple way of doing this is to assign the numbers 0, +1, or +2 to each factor depending on whether they are definitely absent (0), doubtfully present (+1), or clearly present (+2). The numbers assigned to each factor are then summed to provide a total score that can be used to assist decision making. Scored factor systems are frequently used in clinical medicine and in business. They are not normally considered capable of making decisions without human input; they only assist in the deciding process, generally confirming the intuitive perceptions of the user or perhaps focusing attention on the best options. More sophisticated scoring systems can identify the best options even more clearly.[132]

§20. Legal calculus and legal science

If the basic themes of this note are sound, a number of consequences follow which relate to legal theory and writing, professional education in law, testing of legal competence and so on. Most importantly, it should be noted that the study of law is not merely training for the hurly burly of legal practice (like learning to box) but can and should be a scientific enterprise. Scientific enquiry has two main aspects, imagination and formal structure, both of which are necessary. Without creative thinking,

---

[131] DIAGNOSTIC AND STATISTICAL MANUAL OF MENTAL DISORDERS 4th edn. American Psychiatric Association, 1994. p.142. The DSM system is, of course, a great deal more sophisticated than this simple item would suggest.

[132] Early medical diagnostic software was notoriously inaccurate but is currently more sophisticated.

investigation becomes mechanical tinkering, a matter of hit and miss. Without logical ordering, enquiry flounders around and there can be little or no progress or reliable communication between one researcher and another. These considerations apply to legal studies. Bringing lofty objectives and stubborn facts together in workable systems is not a matter for dull and uninventive minds. Likewise since the study of law is a communal or collegial matter, form and method are essential to ensure good communication and generally maintain orderly progress across the entire profession. The development of an organized legal corpus along these lines has always been difficult and is not becoming any easier, but it is as feasible in law as it is elsewhere. If neurosurgeons can devise coma scales to ensure reliable observation of head injured patients and to communicate with one another about treatments and outcomes, a most difficult and complex matter, lawyers should surely be able to develop adequate formal tools for use in the study and practice of law.[133]

§20 Some practical uses of formalism in law

There are a number of other potential benefits which the use of formal methods in legal affairs could be expected to produce.

1. *Improving classroom teaching methods.* From the formalist perspective, it would appear that our basic methodology is flawed. The student prepares by studying the case report and is then expected to find a way through the facts and the opinion to the ruling in the case. In this process the relevant law must be found somewhere, which can be a difficult task given only the usual class materials. If the first item in those materials could be an organized representation of the law, the remaining items, the cases where it was applied, would make more sense. Some might think that it is a good thing to make the student hunt around for this vital information. The extra labor is, however, irrational, like the Egyptians making the Israelites make bricks without

---

[133] I am currently involved with a colleague, Prof. Olivia Weeks, in developing a formal apparatus for North Carolina Products Liability law. This program is well advanced and could be adapted for other states.

straw. Time might be better spent in mastering the appropriate legal apparatus, preferably in a good formal arrangement, and then seeing how it is and should be applied in the assigned cases.[134]

2. *Improving the writing of judicial opinions.* A judicial opinion is intended to explain or justify the processes by which the judge decided the case, but finding this is often very difficult. It has been described a looking for a black cat in a coal cellar on a moonless night when there is no cat there in the first place. Formally the opinion should first identify the area of law in which the case is supposed to sound, then the particular rules (or terms) that are deemed relevant and finally the way in which they were applied to the facts of the case. This formal effort is not needed in every case and perhaps only in important or unusual ones. Easy cases, where the law and its application are obvious will probably not reach the appellate courts and will not therefore be reported. If the result is very obvious the case should not reach the courts at all. Another group of appellate cases, a very large one, will turn on procedural objections (e.g. whether a certain witness should or should not have been allowed to testify) and very little in the way of formal method will be needed here also. Good formal arrangement will be more likely to be required in difficult cases, complex cases and those where the law is being changed or applied in a novel way. At the very least in such cases, the relevant legal terms should be explicitly noted, defined if necessary, and any change or development in the legal apparatus should be clearly and explicitly indicated. It will also probably be of importance in such cases to identify the ends or goals guiding the application of that part of the law and how any conflict between them was resolved. All this is frequently done using the simplest and oldest of formal methods, the "and " and the "or" games deriving from the elements in the forms of action at common law. Decisions where factors are weighed

---

[134]I am of course aware of the benefits of the students learning to respond to questions under fire, a common scenario in the case book method of instruction. But this could be maintained with a more rational method of preparation for class.

and considered do not occur in every case, but where they do, weighted or scored factor games might be helpful to the court, both in the deciding process and in justifying the conclusions in the eyes of others. Algorithms (branching logics), expressing the law in a skeleton format, are useful in two ways. First they act in law, and elsewhere, as check lists, helping to ensure that no important item in the legal apparatus has been overlooked. Second, they are useful as communication devices since they can make very clear to later readers, e.g. by circling or otherwise indicating items, the points on which the attention of the court has been focused. It is not being suggested here that judicial opinions be accompanied by branching diagrams or scored factor lists, though one might ask "why not?. A more acceptable suggestion might be that the judicial clerks accompany their briefs to the judges with formal materials to make it quite clear what they are saying and, incidentally, that they are methodical workers..

3. *Revitalizing legal scholarship.* A senior judicial clerk of many years experience has recently commented that judges no longer cite nor pay much attention to law review articles[135]. Several possible reasons for this fact, if fact it be, could be considered. It is true that many other sources of legal information are now available, such as computer research tools and authoritative publications (Restatements of the Law and Uniform Statutes) but it appears that current legal writing is not helpful to those who are actually in the business of settling and deciding cases. Much of it is focused on individual decisions with comment, largely of a political nature, either bemoaning or approving the direction the law appears to be taking. It is at this point that studies in Descriptive Jurisprudence, employing modern formal logics, could be helpful. These would review an area of law and present analyses of it using formal tools as already described. The branching diagram is particularly useful in comparing rules in different jurisdictions or variants of the same rule,

---

[135] Thomas L Fowler, Law Reviews and Their Relevance to Modern Legal Problems. 24(1) Campbell Law Revierw (2002) 47.

e.g. a traditional version, a radically new version and perhaps a compromise solution. A sample branching diagram can be found in the second appendix following the final chapter (the Ballet of the Books). This represents an area in Products Liability Law. If variations of the relevant law are compared formally this can not only clarify the issues, but also help courts and legislators to make up their mind which of the variant rules they should adopt. Competing policies could also be represented by factor based decisional logical forms. Review articles and relevant chapters in treaties can also be indicated. This kind of formal analysis of existing law (and any proposed changes) would surely be helpful to courts, practicing lawyers and, where appropriate, to legislators

APPENDIX #2
FORMAL PRESENTATION OF AN
AREA IN PRODUCTS LIABILITY LAW

Algorithm of Products Libility law (WC)

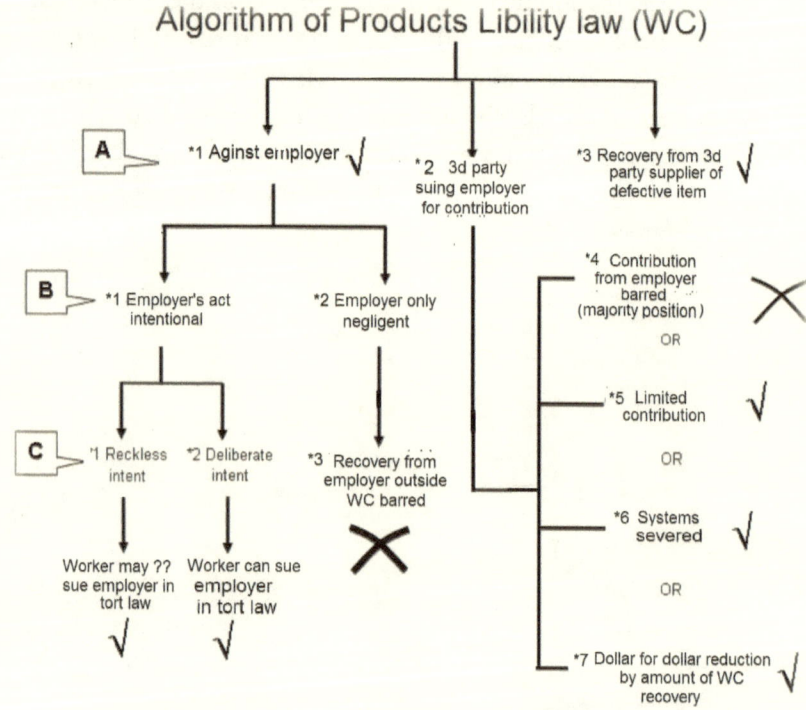

Algorithm applied to Worker's Compensation Law in Products liability

*******ILLUSTRATIVE CASES********

C1 *Wiggins v Pelikan* 513 S.E.2d 829 (1999)

Plaintiff was employed as a slitter in a plant which produced ribbons for computers from large rolls of film. She transported the rolls in a rather top heavy machine which toppled over on her and caused serious spinal injuries. She sued her employer in the intentional tort exception to the Workers' Compensation provisions as laid down in *Woodson v. Rowland*, 407 S.E.2d 222 (1991). At trial the court entered a directed verdict in favor of the employer and plaintiff appealed. In deciding whether the actions of the employer were so reckless as to be tantamount to being deliberate the court used a number of factors When deciding whether a defendant-employer acted with "substantial certainty" of the consequences of its conduct, courts have considered several questions, including the following:

1) Whether the risk that caused the harm existed for a long period of time without causing injury.
2) Whether the risk was created by a defective instrumentality with a high probability of causing the harm
3) Whether there was evidence the employer, prior to the accident, attempted to remedy the risk that caused the harm.
4) Whether the employer's conduct which created the risk violated state or federal work safety regulations.
5) Whether the defendant-employer created a risk by failing to adhere to an industry practice, even though there was no violation of a state or federal safety regulation.
6) Whether the defendant-employer offered training in the safe behavior appropriate in the context of the risk causing the harm.

Of these factors the first, a long record of safe usage, was considered to be particularly important (a major factor?).

Applying these considerations to the present case the court affirmed the directed verdict in favor of the employer.

The case is particularly valuable in that there are numerous references in support of and interpreting each of these factors. But a factor game, especially a weighted one, might well have been appropriate.

C2 Jones v Willamette Industries 463 S.E.2d 294 (1995)

A slag wall collapsed due to cooling, causing injuries to workers. There had been several such accidents over the years and the plaintiffs sued employers outside the Workers Compensation system alleging the intentional tort exception to the exclusivity provisions of the Statute. The trial court had entered a directed verdict in favor of the employer and this was affirmed on appeal, as accidents had been few and there had been no problems for ages and the workers had not even reported some of them.

N.B. For reasons of space, only a few cases have been included here. The purposes and policies served by this part of the law and also references to Law Review articles and other relevant materials have likewise been omitted as they tend to be rather bulky and take up too much space.. It can easily be seen how they could be linked to any particular part of the algorithm]